W9-CMB-513

By Roy Meredith

MR. LINCOLN'S CAMERA MAN MATHEW B. BRADY

THE FACE OF ROBERT E. LEE

MR. LINCOLN'S CONTEMPORARIES

THE AMERICAN WARS

THIS WAS ANDERSONVILLE

STORM OVER SUMTER

MR. LINCOLN'S GENERAL

U. S. GRANT

Grant is the first General I have had.

President ABRAHAM LINCOLN

MR. LINCOLN'S GENERAL

U. S. GRANT

AN ILLUSTRATED AUTOBIOGRAPHY

Edited and Arranged by

Roy Meredith

BONANZA BOOKS, NEW YORK

92
Gra

This edition is published by Bonanza Books,
distributed by Crown Publishers, Inc.,
by arrangement with Roy Meredith.
h g f e d c b a
BONANZA 1981 EDITION

Manufactured in the United States of America

Library of Congress Cataloging in Publication Data

Grant, Ulysses S. (Ulysses Simpson), 1822-1885.
    Mr. Lincoln's general, U.S. Grant.

    Consists largely of literary material drawn
from General Grant's Personal memoirs.
    Reprint. Originally published: New York:
Dutton 1959.
    1. Grant, Ulysses S. (Ulysses Simpson),
1822-1885.   2. United States—History—Civil
War, 1861-1865—Campaigns and battles.
3. Presidents—United States—Biography.
4. Generals—United States—Biography.
5. United States. Army—Biography.
I. Meredith, Roy, 1908–   II. Title.
E672.A352   1981   973.7′3′0924 [B] 81-10036
ISBN 0-517-35299-0   AACR2

TO THE MEMORY OF

MY GRANDFATHER

WILLIAM HENRY CORSA

1843   1925

1st NEW YORK, LINCOLN

CAVALRY

ARMY OF THE POTOMAC

1861   1865

Contents

Preface

ULYSSES S. GRANT—fighting general—one of the few leaders of the Civil War who really understood how the Civil War should be fought! What a shame that every schoolboy does not remember General Grant for this reason. The phenomena of myth and misinformation persist throughout the years, even though historians have recorded the facts. Instead of a man of action, there still remains the picture of drunkard; instead of a great military strategist, there still exists the picture of butcher and bungler. General Grant *was* a strange man: introspective, modest, shy, all of which are odd characteristics for a military man—a man of action.

It is interesting to me how little attention is paid to Grant's great military achievements. The magic name of Gettysburg, for instance, puts a name like Fort Donelson in the shadow; and yet, the capture of Fort Donelson, accomplished by Grant, was one of the truly great victories of the Civil War that happened in the early stages, long before Eastern victories. The capture of Donelson was the first weakening of the control of the Confederacy in the West. The Eastern theater had hardly begun, but the Confederate cause was lost with the loss of the Mississippi Valley.

The capture of Vicksburg, another brilliant campaign, engineered and carried out by Grant, split the Confederacy in two and was the beginning of the end for the Southern cause. Vicksburg, along with places like Corinth, Pittsburgh Landing, and Shiloh, was to be the foundation upon which the monumental structure of the bloody years to follow rested. Ulysses S. Grant was the early architect.

Unfortunately, a portion of history is written by men who have an ax to grind. In the early days of the war, there was much rivalry, political, military and egotistical. Men like General Henry W. Halleck, Chief of Staff, and Leonard Swett wrote letters, filled with envy, condemning Grant and giving him no credit. Too often, regardless of later scholarship and research, the damage of these letters persists.

Lincoln, however, understood that Grant knew what had to be done. Perhaps this is because Grant's actions and writing coincided with the President's views. Up to this time they had never met, but Grant, for instance, never recognized the Confederate states and wrote about them as states in rebellion. This was the cornerstone upon which Lincoln built his attitude. Both men, without communicating with each other, said that no state had a right to secede, and as such, the claim of the Southern states of having seceded was disallowed. They were states in rebellion! Grant and Lincoln never wavered in this attitude. It was one of the things which infuriated Jefferson Davis, in that he was not recognized by either of these men as President of the Confederacy, but only as a participant in rebellion.

All of the actions of Grant and his understanding of how the war had to be fought hardly seem to be the attitude of a drunkard. Lincoln understood the war, and as such, saw the great contributions that were made by Grant. When he put him in charge of the Army of the Potomac, this was recognition and was part of the answer to the many malicious charges brought against Grant, grown out of jealousy of his genius. When those who were shocked at this appointment brought up the old "drinking question" to Lincoln, he said, "I can't spare this man, he fights."

Up to the time that Grant was put in charge of the Army of the Potomac, this fine army, misguided by one general after another, had retreated or had stood frozen watching the Confederate army retreat. It stood as if relieved that Mr. Lee had not overrun them. It stood mute and content, watching the enemy leave the field, allowing them to refurbish, refresh and rebuild—to come out and fight another day. Mr. Grant changed all this; this same army was soon to become the pursuer, soon to be the army to take the initiative rather than to be constantly on the defensive. Grant indeed recognized that the army taking the offensive would win the war sooner, even though the price to pay would be terrible, indeed.

The pictures in this book have been collected with the same loving care that Mr. Meredith showed in his earlier book *Mr. Lincoln's Camera Man, Mathew B. Brady*. They are great pictures, indeed, and have been reproduced sharply and with an eye to having a personality emerge, rather than just the mere recording of antique photographs. The captions under the pictures are, in many instances, in the words of Grant himself. From this marvelous combination, there emerges a true picture of the real Grant.

This book, I think, will do much to put Ulysses S. Grant back into his proper perspective. It will, I hope, help accomplish what history has more or less not been able to do: to correct a popular opinion which is in error. It would be a great contribution to history if the facts be separated from the fancy and, once for all, diminish the evil myths surrounding a great man.

WILLIAM KALAND

Introduction

GENERAL ULYSSES SIMPSON GRANT, like Sherman, Sheridan, McPherson, Porter, Farragut, and a few others, was one of that small but excellent school of military and naval officers who made up the hard core of the Army and Navy during the Civil War. Their firm, practical grasp of their calling set them distinctly apart from the wire-pullers, glory-seekers, incompetents, and self-seeking political generals, who, having little or no military talent, resorted to cupidity, bluff, and undercover politics to further their personal ambitions.

Charles Anderson Dana, Assistant Secretary of War in Mr. Lincoln's Cabinet, took particular notice of this when he visited General Grant's headquarters sometime after the Battle of Shiloh. He mentioned the names of three remarkable men, whose lack of guile and of jealousy and whose devotion to duty above personal ambition made a great impression on his mind. Grant, Sherman, and McPherson, "in their unpretending simplicity," he wrote, "were alike as three peas."

In contrast to today's popular conception of General Grant as soldier and President is the simple fact that General Grant was indeed one of America's greatest soldiers; a punctilious gentleman of scrupulous honesty and quiet and profound ability.

A product of the American West, Grant was a man without guile, who never uttered an oath in his life no matter how compelling the circumstances. Passionately devoted to his family, Grant's first thought was always of their welfare, and when he was away from them for any length of time he was lonely and miserable.

Within the realm of military affairs, where matters had to be right or wrong, black or white, with the resulting consequences, Grant was superb, a careful thinker of mathematical precision, able instinctively to divine the enemy's intentions and plan accordingly. His campaigns are simple testimony to this. From the moment he took command of the Army of the Tennessee, his quiet confidence was felt throughout the entire army.

Outside that realm, Grant had neither the equipment, mental sagacity, nor the inclination to take part in the rough game of practical politics, where matters were not what they seemed to be on the surface. In this chameleon-like atmosphere, Grant was completely out of his element, not because of any shortcomings in education, ability, or acumen, but because he was simply unable to see any virtue in a consistency which impeded progress or set man against man. Eminently successful as a soldier, and in military diplomacy and scholarship, Grant possessed that unusual quality of fairness, of seeing the good on both sides, which is sure death to any American politician.

As for his failures and setbacks in business, which many of his contemporaries have made much of, the answer can be summed up in one sentence: Grant was too honorable a man to conceive of dishonor in his friends. Grant had the fatal loyalty of believing in a friend "long after others had given him up."

But Grant had no patience with clever rascals, shrewd politicians, starry-eyed reformers, or incompetents who sought political office for personal gain and aggrandizement, and because of this he made many enemies. Grant had an inborn instinct and will to give honest public service, and worked hard to achieve results. But Grant hated politics of all kinds, and felt about the Presidency as did General Sherman who refused to run for the office.

"I did not want the Presidency," said General Grant, in a conversation with his friend John Russell Young, long after his two terms in office were ended, "and have never quite forgiven myself for resigning the command of the army to accept it; but it could not be helped. I owed my honors and opportunities to the Republican Party, and if my name could aid it I was bound to accept. The second nomination was almost due to me—if I may use a phrase—because of the bitterness of political and personal opponents. My re-election was a great gratification because it showed me how the country felt . . . but personally I was weary of the office. I never wanted to get out of a place as much as I did to get out of the Presidency. . . ."

When, on April 15, 1861, President Lincoln called on the militia of the loyal States to furnish seventy-five thousand men "to suppress combinations . . . too powerful to be suppressed by the ordinary course of judicial proceedings," there was no general staff, no plan, and there were no organized services of any kind. The regular army of thirteen thousand men of all arms, officers and men, was to be kept intact, and to the governors of the various northern States fell the burden and responsibility of preparing the willing but undisciplined volunteers.

These men had to be supplied ordnance, small arms, rifles, and ammunition, and in the wake of Lincoln's call for volunteers came the "reign of shoddy," thievish contractors and peddlers of "influence," politicians who had given quick readings to Napoleon's campaigns and to Jomini on *The Art of War,* and ex-militia captains who would not be satisfied with less than a general's star.

By way of contrast, in Galena, Illinois, Grant walked out of his father's store, never to return, when news of President Lincoln's call for troops was received. With combat experience received in the Mexican War as a graduate lieutenant of West Point, Grant sought nothing but to serve his country in any capacity in which he could be helpful.

"When I was in St. Louis the year before Lincoln's election," he once said to his friend John Russell Young, "it made my blood run cold to hear friends of mine, Southern men—as many of my friends were—deliberately discuss the dissolution of the Union as though it were a tariff bill. I could not endure it. The very thought of it was pain. I wanted to leave the country if disunion was accomplished. I could not have lived in the country. It was this feeling that impelled me to volunteer. I was a poor man with a family. I never thought of commands or battles. I only wanted to fight for the Union. That feeling carried me through the war. I never felt any special pleasure in my promotions. I was naturally glad when they came. But I never thought of it. The only promotion I ever rejoiced in was when I was made a major general in the regular army. I was happy over that, because it made me the *junior* major general, and I hoped, when the war was over, that I could live in California. I had been yearning for the opportunity to return to California, and I saw it in that promotion. When I was given a higher command, I was sorry, because it involved a residence in Washington, which, at that time, of all places in the country I disliked, and it dissolved my hopes of a return to the Pacific coast. I came to like Washington, however, when I knew it. My only feeling in the war was a desire to see it over and the rebellion suppressed. It never entered my head, for instance, to consider the terms we should take from the South if beaten. I never heard Mr. Lincoln allude to such a thing, and I do not think he ever considered it."

Grant's views on war differed greatly from the German and French military strategists von Clausewitz and Napoleon. Napoleon's books and maxims were read assiduously by most of the Union generals, and in the Confederate army Stonewall Jackson always carried a book of Napoleon's maxims on war in his saddlebags. Grant's comments on war in general and generals in particular are interesting and shrewd. "War," he said, "is progressive, because all the instruments and elements of war are progressive. I do not believe in luck in war any more than luck in business. Luck is a small matter, and may affect a battle or a movement, but not a campaign or a career . . . there is nothing ideal in war."

Grant's estimate of the generals of both sides, North and South, is equally astute. "In the popular estimate of generals," wrote Grant, "nothing succeeds but success . . . it is difficult to know what constitutes a great general. Some of our generals failed because they lost the confidence of the country in trying to win the confidence of the politicians. Some of them failed, like Hooker at Chancellorsville, because when they won a victory they lost their heads, and did not know what to do with it. Some of our generals failed because they worked out everything by rule . . . they knew what Frederick did at one place, and Napoleon at another. They were always thinking about what Napoleon would do. Unfortunately for their plans, the rebels would be thinking about something else. I don't under-

[15]

rate the value of military knowledge, but men who make war in slavish observance of rules will fail."

General Robert E. Lee enjoyed universal fame during the Civil War, especially in Europe where his reputation as the South's greatest general had grown with every battle. The Northern newspapers, promoting this fame to the detriment and embarrassment of the Union generals, reported that the contest was uneven and unfair to the South; that the South gained her victories by great generalship, valor, and chivalry; the North by overwhelming brute force. Heretofore, every Union general who faced Lee had been defeated by an army nearly half the size of his own, with inferior equipment and meager resources. Psychologically, the great myth of invincibility which had been built up around Lee by the Northern press had been a mental hazard to the Union generals and affected their operations.

Grant had no such illusions about Lee, and exploded the myth into thin air, saying: "I never ranked Lee as high as some others of the army, that is to say, I never had as much anxiety when he was in my front as when Joe Johnston was in front. Lee was a good man, a fair commander, who had everything in his favor. He was a man who needed sunshine. He was supported by a large party in the North; he had the support and sympathy of the outside world. All this is of immense advantage to a general. Lee had this in remarkable degree. Everything he did was right. He was treated like a demi-god. Our generals had a hostile press, lukewarm friends, and a public opinion outside."

Never before (or since) has a war been "covered" by the press with more freedom or license. American newspaper editors were still in the Webb-Bennett era of irresponsibility; the national interest was to them whatever they, as individuals, might think it was. Their correspondents and artists swarmed over the battlefields, using government supplies and equipment, preëmpting government transportation, and telegraphing back their findings or imaginings, sometimes of the most confidential material, with utter disregard of practical consequences. Grant and Sherman took no stock in newspaper correspondents; in fact, they abominated all newspaper activity. Army headquarters, as far as Grant and Sherman were concerned, was "off limits" to all newspaper men, and they could never understand how Pope, Burnside, McClellan, and Hooker could have become influenced by newspapers, especially when it came to military evaluations.

While Grant respected Lee as a man, he was not awed by Lee's austerity or military qualifications. "Lee was of a slow, conservative, cautious nature, without imagination or humor, always the same, with grave dignity," said Grant. "I never could see in his achievements what justifies his reputation. The illusion that nothing but heavy odds beat him will not stand up in the ultimate light of history. I know it is not true. Lee was a good deal of a headquarters general; a desk general from what I hear, and from what his officers say. He was almost too old for active service—the best service in the field. At the time of the surrender he was fifty-eight or fifty-nine and I was forty-three. His officers used to say that he posed himself, that he was retiring and exclusive, and that his headquarters were difficult of access. I remember, when the commissioners came through our lines to treat, just before the surrender, that one of them remarked on the great difference between our headquarters and Lee's. I always kept open house at headquarters, as far as the army was concerned."

The delicate sensibilities and high purposes of Lee were visibly shaken when he received news of Grant's appointment to the supreme command of the Federal armies. There were many disagreeable things that confronted Lee in Virginia, but this news was the most disagreeable of all. Lee had undoubtedly been following the audacious and successful campaigns of Grant in the West, and knew that he would now be facing a shrewd and tenacious fighter who would not give up easily. Speaking of Grant's appointment to his officers, Lee said, "We must make up our minds to get into line of battle and to stay there, for that man will fight us every day and every hour till the end of the war." Such was Lee's estimate of the new Union commander with whom he would have to match wits in the desperate months to come when the Army of Northern Virginia would be fighting for its very life on the old battlegrounds of its former triumphs.

To General Grant, soldiering was a noble and demanding profession that belonged to the young, especially applying to combat officers, and was of paramount importance to the success of any campaign. "A successful general needs health and youth and energy," he said. "I should not like to put a general in the field over fifty. When I was in the army I had a physique that could stand anything. Whether I slept on the ground or in a tent, whether I slept one hour or ten in twenty-four, whether I had one meal or three, or none, made no difference. I could lie down and sleep in the rain without caring . . . the power to endure is an immense power, and naturally belongs to youth."

Speaking of his own military campaigns, Grant was his own severest critic, and it is in these statements and reminiscences that Grant reveals the formidable reasons behind his success in the field. His strength of character and military prowess shine all the more brightly when his campaigns are considered in the light of the handicaps, political and military, under which they were conducted. And despite the fact that Grant disliked both war and the boredom of military life during peacetime, he had found new faith in himself after the fall of Fort Sumter.

Having taken a colonelcy in a regiment of Illinois volunteers, he forgot all the snubs and rebuffs he had suffered since his resignation from the regular army under charges of drunkenness. Forgotten, too, were his aimless driftings from job to job, from failure to failure. Grant, after his successful campaign against the Confederate partisans in Missouri, was made a brigadier general in the fall of 1861. His innate strategic sense told him that the Tennessee and Cumberland rivers were avenues that led deep into the economic body of the South, broad areas untouched by war that supplied and armed the Confederate armies, and he wrung from his dubious superior, General Henry Wager Halleck, permission to reduce the forts which commanded those rivers. During his well planned operations against Fort Henry and Fort Donelson, Grant was hampered by officers who tried their utmost to have him removed because his abilities, by comparison, outshone their own. But Grant's dominating characteristic was a singleness of purpose and a desire for action, and few officers, with the exceptions of Sherman and McPherson, were to be found with anything approaching these qualities. For Grant, in the early days of the war, it was a question of too many of the wrongs and too little of the rights. Ignoring the strange machinations of jealousy on the part of McClernand and Halleck, whose cupidity and sly efforts to discredit him amounted to sheer genius, Grant kept on with the job in hand, quietly and surely.

The "stars in their courses" were fighting with Grant, and after his "unconditional surrender" terms at Donelson, Grant's advance rolled on and halted at Pittsburg Landing on the Tennessee, its rear to the swollen river and its front uncovered. Halleck had plans of his own; and so Grant's army was left open to a sudden attack in force. The result was bloody Shiloh, Grant's army holding fast at a cost of thirteen thousand killed, wounded, and missing.

After the Battle of Shiloh, the newspapers reported erroneously that Grant and his army had been "surprised," that Grant's men "were killed over their coffee." "There was no surprise about it," said General Grant to John Russell Young, with a smile, "except, perhaps, to the newspaper correspondents. . . . I was so satisfied with the result, and so certain that I would beat Beauregard, even without Buell's aid, that I went in person to each division commander and ordered an advance along the line at four in the morning. Shiloh was one of the most important battles of the war. It was there that our Western soldiers first met the enemy in a pitched battle. From that day they never feared to fight the enemy, and never went into action without feeling sure they would win . . . Sherman was the hero of Shiloh."

Grant felt that he had made fewer mistakes in the Vicksburg campaign than in any other campaign he conducted. From his point of view the battle of Cold Harbor, in Virginia, should never have been fought. But if he had to fight Vicksburg over again, he would fight it the same way. "If the Vicksburg campaign," said General Grant, "meant anything in a military point of view, it was that there are no fixed laws of war which are not subject to the conditions of the country, the climate, and the habits of the people. The laws of successful war in one generation would insure defeat in another. I was well served in the Vicksburg campaign."

Vicious rumor had it, after the fall of Vicksburg, that General John B. Pemberton, a Northerner by birth, having surrendered Vicksburg, betrayed the South, especially so when it was surrendered on July Fourth. General Richard Taylor, it was said, made the accusation. Grant came immediately to Pemberton's defense. "Pemberton could not have held Vicksburg a day longer than he did. But desperate as his condition was, he did not want to surrender it. He knew, that as a Northern man by birth, he was under suspicion; that a surrender would have been treated as disloyalty, and rather than incur that reproach he was willing to stand my assault. But as I learned afterwards his officers, and even his men, saw how mad would have been such a course, and he reluctantly accepted the inevitable. I could have carried Vicksburg by assault, and was ready when the surrender took place."

To General Grant the duty of a soldier is to destroy his enemy as quickly as possible, but useless killing that would serve no purpose was as repugnant to him as war itself. At Vicksburg, where further resistance was useless under the circumstances, Grant would have dealt severely with Pemberton had he compelled an assault. "It would have been little less than murder, not only of my men, but of his own. I would severely punish any officer who, under the circumstances, compelled a wanton loss of life. War is war, and murder is murder, and Vicksburg was so far reduced, and its condition so hopeless when it surrendered, that the loss of another life in defending it would have been criminal."

One of the remarkable things about the Southern rebellion was the amazing similarity of views that Grant and President Lincoln held of it. Both saw the war as an illegal uprising or rebellion against the lawful government of the United States. Nor did Grant or Lincoln ever acknowledge the existence of a nation called the Confederate States of America, something which angered not a little the President of the Confederacy, Jefferson Davis. To Grant it was always "the so-called Confederate States;" to Lincoln it was "the States in rebellion." Nothing angered Lincoln more than General Meade's telegram after the Battle of Gettysburg. "We have swept the enemy from our soil," he wired to the President. To which Mr. Lincoln commented heatedly: "Will our generals never get that idea out of their heads? The whole country is our soil!"

It was Grant's "unconditional surrender" demand to General Buckner that brought Grant to the attention of Lincoln. But word had also reached the President about Grant's drinking at headquarters, and Mr. Lincoln wanted to know more about this general who had a habit of winning victories and who, according to reports, was a habitual drinker. Grant's jealous enemies had made the most of a minor weakness and had expanded it out of all proportion. They pressured Lincoln into removing Grant from his command.

Murat Halstead, editor of the *Cincinnati Gazette,* went so far as to write downright lies in a letter to Secretary Salmon P. Chase. "How is it that Grant," he wrote, "who was behind at Fort Henry, drunk at Donelson, surprised at Shiloh, and driven back from Oxford, Miss., is still in command? Governor Chase, these things are true. Our noble army of the Mississippi is being wasted by the foolish, drunken, stupid Grant. He cannot organize or control or fight an army. I have no personal feeling about it; but I know he is an ass. There is not among the whole list of retired major generals a man who is not Grant's superior." Chase endorsed the letter and sent it on to Lincoln, but the President wanted to find out for himself, and asked General John M. Thayer, a caller at the White House, "just in from Vicksburg," to see him.

"General," asked the President, "you have a man down there by the name of Grant, have you not?"

"Yes, sir, we have," was the reply.

"What kind of fellow is he," asked the President.

Thayer replied that Grant was an excellent and popular commander with the army and had a stubborn determination to win under all circumstances.

"Does Grant ever get drunk?" asked Mr. Lincoln bluntly.

"No, Mr. President," replied Thayer, "Grant does not get drunk."

"Is he in the habit of using liquor?" pressed the President.

"I have seen him often, sometimes daily," was the reply, "and I have never noticed the slightest indication of his using any kind of liquor. . . . The charge is atrocious, wickedly false. I saw him repeatedly during the battles of Donelson and Shiloh, on the field, and if there were any sober men on the field, Grant was one of them. . . . I am glad to bring this testimony to you in justice to a much maligned man."

Mr. Lincoln then said: "What I want is generals who will fight battles and win victories. Grant has done this and I propose to stand by him. . . . Somehow I have always felt a leaning toward Grant. Ever since he sent that message to Buckner, 'No terms but unconditional surrender,' I have felt that he was the man that I could tie to, though I have never seen him."

Much has been made of Grant's drinking, and his alleged prowess with the bottle has become legendary. Most of the so-called "facts" concerning this legend were originated by men who disliked Grant intensely because they found that they could not use him. At one time or another, these self-appointed guardians of the public's morals incurred Grant's displeasure, and they turned to discrediting him by grasping the first means at hand—a weakness they expanded out of all proportion.

Judging from the various accounts of Grant's tippling, one would be led to believe that among the officers and men of the army, Grant was the only man who ever tasted liquor. And in this instance, nothing could be more fitting than the ancient adage, "He who would cast the first stone . . ." Grant did drink and, being human, he sometimes overindulged his weakness. Grant grew up in a community of hardy backwoodsmen and farmers to whom liquor was no stranger; not to mention the fact that it was a hard-drinking army that went into Mexico, when Grant, as a young lieutenant, away from his bride-to-be and out of sympathy with the war and the boredom of military life, drank occasionally to relieve that boredom. Perhaps Grant's liking for liquor was hereditary; his grandfather, Noah, a captain in the Revolution, was a heavy drinker, but in spite of everything Grant ignored the prattlings and tattlings against him and kept at the job in hand.

Mr. Lincoln kept his word and stuck by his brilliant field commander. His own secretaries, John G. Nicolay and John Hay, noted that when busybodies and talebearers accused Grant of overindulgence, Lincoln would always reply: "If I knew what brand of whisky he drinks I would send a barrel or so to some other generals."

But Grant had an answer for his detractors: "Visitors to the camps went home with dismal stories to relate (of rain, mud, fever, measles, and small-pox); Northern newspapers came back to the soldiers with these stories exaggerated. Because I would not divulge my ultimate plans to visitors, they pronounced me idle, incompetent and unfit to command men in an emergency, and clamored for my removal. Not to be satisfied, many named who my successor should be. McClernand, Frémont, Hunter, and McClellan were all mentioned in this connection." When Lincoln was again put under pressure to remove Grant on the grounds that he had been wasteful of his men, Mr. Lincoln replied: "I can't spare this man; he fights."

Shortly before the fall of Vicksburg, public feeling against Grant began to change, and this change was not lost on General Sherman, who idolized Grant. In a letter home he wrote: "Grant is now deservedly the hero. He is entitled to all the credit. . . . He is now belabored by praise by those who a month ago accused him of all the sins in the calendar, and who next week will turn against him if so blows the popular breeze. Vox populi, vox humbug!"

One thing that Grant had in abundance was self-confidence, and never was that confidence more prominently displayed than when he was given the supreme command of the Union armies. After the Battle of Gettysburg, Grant was offered the command of the Army of the Potomac, but he managed "to keep out of it." He had seen all the political maneuvering he cared to, and had seen many generals fall, one after another, "like bricks in a row," and he shrank from it. He had seen the need for coordination of all the Union armies early in the war, but because of the political situation he hesitated to suggest it. When the bill creating the grade of Lieutenant General was proposed for him, he wrote to his friend Congressman E. B. Washburne, opposing it. Though he did not want it, he later found that "the bill was right" and he was wrong.

"When I took command of the army," said General Grant on one occasion to John Russell Young, "I had a dream that I tried to realize—to re-unite and re-create the whole army. I talked it over with Sherman. Sherman and I knew so many fine, brave officers. We knew them in West Point and the army. We had the sympathy of former comradeship. Neither Sherman nor I had been in any way concerned in Eastern troubles, and we knew that there were no better soldiers in the army than some of those who were under a cloud with Mr. Stanton. Then I wanted to make the war as national as possible, to bring in all parties. I was anxious specially to conciliate and recognize the Democratic element. The country belonged as well to the Democrats as to us, and I did not believe in a Republican war. I felt that we needed every musket and every sword to put down the rebellion. So when I came East I came prepared and anxious to assign McClellan, Buell, and others to command. I had confidence in their ability and loyalty, confidence which, notwithstanding our differences in politics, has never faltered. But I was disappointed. . . . The generals were not in a humor to be conciliated. I soon saw my plan was not feasible, and gave it up. . . . I have always regretted that. We had work for everybody during the war, for those especially who knew the business. What interfered with our officers more than anything else was allowing themselves a political bias."

Grant took command of the Army of the Potomac and commenced operations, and by May of 1864 all the Union armies were in motion. The North was shocked by what followed, but the South was crushed by it. "I will agree to be there [Richmond] in about four days," said Grant to an inquisitive reporter, "that is, if General Lee becomes a party to the agreement; but if he objects, the trip will undoubtedly be prolonged." Grant's great campaign of 1864–1865 was a coördinated operation between the army and navy. The story of that campaign is told by Grant himself in his *Memoirs* that follow.

There are, however, one or two incidents worth telling for an intimate picture of General Grant in the last year of the war. One day, near the end of the war, at City Point headquarters, one of Grant's officers asked, "Why don't you ask the President to come down and visit you?" Grant replied that Mr. Lincoln was in command of the army and could come whenever he wished. It was then brought to Grant's attention that the main reason Lincoln had not come was the talk about his interference with the generals in the field and his reluctance to impose himself on them. Grant at once telegraphed to Washington and invited Mr. Lincoln to visit the army at City Point.

"He came at once," said General Grant. "He was really most anxious to see the army, and be with it in its final struggle. It was an immense relief to him to be away from Washington. He remained at my headquarters until Richmond was taken. He entered Richmond, and I went after Lee."

Grant was pleased and happy that President Lincoln had spent most of his last days at City Point. "Lincoln, I may say, spent the last days of his life with me. I often recall those days," said General Grant. ". . . He lived on a dispatch-boat in the river, but he was always around headquarters. He was a fine horseman, and rode my horse Cincinnati. We visited the different camps, and I did all that I could to interest him. He was very anxious about the war closing; was afraid we could not stand a new campaign, and wanted to be around when the crash came. I have no doubt that Lincoln will be a conspicuous figure of the war; one of the great figures of history. He was a great man, a very great man. The more I saw of him, the more this impressed me. He was incontestably the greatest man I ever knew. . . ."

Grant's apprehension of Lee's escaping him after Petersburg had fallen was a bit of military information Lee could have used to advantage had he known about it at the time. "My anxiety for some time before Richmond fell was lest Lee should abandon it," said Grant. "I was in a position of extreme difficulty. I was marching away from my supplies, while Lee was falling back on his supplies. If Lee had continued his flight another day, I should have had to abandon my pursuit, fall back to Danville, build the railroad and feed my army. So far as supplies were concerned, I was almost at my last gasp when the surrender took place." After the Reconstruction had begun, an allusion was made to the feeling in the South that Jefferson Davis had done the South an injury, that he had not done his best for the Confederacy. There were many attacks on Davis afterward, when the "might-have-beens" were being bandied about by the Southern press. Grant felt that Davis had done all he could for the South and that there was nothing in his administration that showed that he was false "to his side" or "feeble in defending it." Grant believed that Davis was entitled to all the honors for "gallantry and persistence." "The South fell because it was defeated," said Grant. "Lincoln destroyed it, not Davis."

The South, in the years after the war, was a disappointment to General Grant. After Lee had surrendered, Grant was more than willing to meet the South more than halfway in a spirit of conciliation, but the South would have none of it. "They have not forgotten the war," he said, sadly.

"Looking back over the whole policy of reconstruction, it seems to me that the wisest thing would have been to continue for some time the military rule. Sensible Southern men see now that there was no government so frugal, so just and fair as what they had under our generals. That would have enabled the Southern people to pull themselves together and repair material losses. As to depriving them, even for a time, of suffrage, that was our right as conquerors, and it would have been a mild penalty for the stupendous crime of treason. . . ."

General Grant's last years, following his two terms in the Presidency, were years of painful illness. The dreaded cancer had attacked his throat, and medical science of the time was unable to relieve his suffering. He had been frequently urged by friends to write his memoirs. He had never thought of writing anything for publication until the editor of the *Century Magazine* asked him to write a few articles on the war for him. At the age of sixty-two, an injury received from a fall confined him to his home, and he took this opportunity for the pleasant pastime of study. For the money it gave him, Grant agreed to do the articles, as he was living on borrowed money. He found the work "congenial," and determined to continue it.

The first volume of the *Memoirs* and a portion of the second was written before he realized that he was in a critical condition. At the time, he was living at Mount MacGregor, New York, near Saratoga Springs. The disease was rapidly running its deadly course, and he was in constant pain. But even in these moments of great suffering, he never spoke unkindly to anyone. To his faithful servant, Harrison, he talked about his book. His greatest fear was that he should die before it was completed. "I have been awake nearly all night thinking about my book. If that were only finished I should be content."

At this stage of his illness, his voice scarcely audible above a whisper, the sick soldier was more concerned for his family than for himself and, unwilling to cause them any anxiety, feigned sleep when members of the family entered his bedroom. During the months of July and August, he sat on the porch of his house, his throat bandaged, completely absorbed in his work, writing, writing, writing. Nothing touched him more deeply than the spectacle of the crowds of well-wishers who affectionately gathered about his door to inquire about his condition. They come by train, carriage, and on foot from the railway station, some walking silently past the house, some waving, others raising their hats in salutation. Letters and telegrams came pouring in from Sheridan, Schofield, Joe Johnston, and Longstreet, and he was gratified that "people, both North and South," were "equally kind in their expressions of sympathy." General Buckner, a member of the same graduating class as Grant, spent an hour talking with him, Grant writing his replies with a pencil, his speech having failed. During that interview with his Fort Donelson adversary and former classmate at West Point, Grant wrote: "I have seen since my sickness, just what I have wished to see ever since the war—harmony and good feeling among the sections." The closing days of General Grant were grievously sad.

On July 2, 1885, General Grant, while seated on the porch of his house, handed his physician, Dr. Douglas, a note which he had just penciled: "I ask you not to show this to anyone, unless the physicians you consult with, until the end. Particularly, I want it kept from my family. If it is known to one man, the papers will get it, and they [his family] will get it. It would only distress them beyond endurance to know it. . . . I would say, therefore, to you and your colleagues, to make me as comfortable as you can. If it is within God's providence that I should go now, I am ready to obey his call without a murmur."

Dr. Douglas tried to encourage the general, but a few days later Grant again penciled another note: "After all, however, the disease is still there, and must be fatal in the end. My life is precious, of course, to my family, and would be to me if I could recover entirely. . . . I first wanted so many days to work on my book, so that the authorship would be clearly mine. . . . My work had been done so hastily that much was left out, and I did it all over again, from the crossing of the James River, in June, 1864, to Appomattox, in 1865. Since then I have added some fifty pages to the book, there is nothing more that I should do to it now, and therefore I am not likely to be more ready to go than at this moment."

General Grant's prayer that the end would soon relieve him of his cruelly agonizing pain was soon granted, but not before his most fervent wish, that he should live to finish his book, was gratified. "Of course, I am sorry to leave my family and friends," he said, sadly, "but I shall be glad to go." A short while later he remarked, "Yes, I have many friends here, and I also have many friends on the other side of the River who have crossed before me," adding, after a brief pause, "it is my wish that they may not have long to wait for me, but that the end will come soon."

He made several rallies in the few days that followed, but there was much physical suffering, borne in silence and patience. Finally, on Thursday, July 23, 1885, General Ulysses S. Grant, "Man of Iron," American soldier and ex-President, surrounded by members of his family, passed away peacefully. His last distinct words were: "I hope no one will feel distressed on my account—"

This book consists largely of literary material drawn from General Grant's brilliant autobiography, supplemented with the most authentic pictures, drawings, and photographs available, and dealing directly with each portion of this remarkable text. Through the combined media of word and picture, although each element is self-contained, I have tried to present to the reader the main course of events in the early life and military campaigns of one of America's greatest soldiers.

Taken together, in their natural chronological sequence, it is hoped that this pictorial technique will present not only the principal actors and events described by the author, but the scene as well. The central theme is, of course, the military career of General Grant as a soldier in the Mexican War, and as a commanding general in the American Civil War.

Grant is the chief narrator throughout. And it is here that I must say a word about the text. In my considered opinion, General Grant's military autobiography is, unequivocally, the finest narrative of its kind ever written. Beyond a doubt, in a superb, captivating style, often with wry touches of humor, as it unfolds, it gives the lie to those who made the malicious claim that General John A. Rawlins, Grant's aide, wrote all Grant's orders, letters, and reports. By no stretch of the imagination could Rawlins have written them. Moreover, Rawlin's influence on Grant during the war has been greatly exaggerated. It is doubtful if many books in the course of history have ever been written under similar conditions. Every word written by this undaunted soldier was accompanied by the severest kind of physical pain. Unwilling to leave his family destitute, he hoped that the results of his extraordinary labors would secure their future.

From the moment he put the first word on paper, Grant knew that it was to be a race with time. His characteristic determination to complete his work before death claimed him was the same as it had been when he faced Lee's army in the Wilderness in the perilous summer of 1864. He would "fight it out on this line if it took all summer." To the great astonishment of his family, physician, publishers, and friends, Grant completed his task, but with little time to spare. It was one of the greatest exhibitions of pluck and perseverance ever witnessed, and his family and close friends were justifiably proud of his accomplishment.

The success of his book was preordained. The sale, in advance of publication, exceeded a quarter of a million copies. The critics made some slights about Grant's grammar, but his friend Mark Twain had a ready reply: "There is about the sun which makes us forget his spots; and when we think of Grant our pulses quicken and his grammar vanishes. We only remember that this is a simple soldier who, all untaught of the silken phrase-makers, linked words together with an art surpassing the art of the schools, and put them into something which will bring to American ears, as long as America shall last, the roll of his vanished drums and the tread of his marching hosts."

ROY MEREDITH

New York, May, 1959

[26]

PART ONE

Of war I sing, war worse than civil, waged over the plains of Emathia, and of legality conferred on crime; I tell how an imperial people turned their victorious hands against their own vitals; how kindred fought against kindred; how, when the compact of tyranny was shattered, all the forces of the shaken world contended to make mankind guilty; how standards confronted hostile standards, eagles were matched against each other, and pilum threatened pilum. What madness was this, my countrymen?

LUCAN (Marcus Annaeus Lucanus)
44 B.C. in The Civil Wars (Pharsalia)

Birthplace of Ulysses S. Grant
Point Pleasant, Clermont County, Ohio

CHAPTER I

"A Noun Is the Name of a Thing."

I WAS born on the 27th of April, 1822, at Point Pleasant, Clermont County, Ohio. In the fall of 1823 we moved to Georgetown, the County seat of Brown, the adjoining county east. This place remained my home until, at the age of seventeen, in 1839, I went to West Point. The schools, at the time of which I write, were very indifferent. There were no free schools, and none in which the scholars were classified. They were all supported by subscription, and a single teacher, often a man or a woman incapable of teaching much, would have thirty or forty scholars, male and female, from the infant learning A B C's up to the young lady of eighteen and the boy of twenty, studying the highest branches taught—the three R's, "Reading, 'Riting, and 'Rithmetic."

I never saw an algebra, or other mathematical works higher than the arithmetic, until after I was appointed to West Point. I then bought a work on algebra in Cincinnati; but having no teacher it was Greek to me.

My life in Georgetown was uneventful. From the age of five or six until seventeen I attended the subscription schools of the village, except during the winters of 1836–7 and 1838–9. The former period was spent in Maysville, Kentucky, attending the school of Richardson and Rand; the latter in Ripley, Ohio, at a private school. I was not studious in habit, and probably did not make progress enough to compensate for the outlay for board and tuition.

At all events, both winters were spent in going over the same old arithmetic, which I knew every word of before, and repeating: "A Noun Is The Name of a Thing."

My father, Jesse Grant

My father was, from my earliest recollection, in comfortable circumstances, considering the times, his place of residence, and the
community in which he lived. Mindful of his own lack of facilities
for acquiring an education, his greatest desire in maturer years was
for the education of his children. Consequently, I never missed a
quarter from school from the time I was old enough to attend 'till
the time of leaving home. This did not exempt me from labor. In
my early days everyone labored, more or less, in the region where my
youth was spent, and more in proportion to their private means. It
was only the very poor who were exempt.

While my father carried on the manufacture of leather and worked
at the trade himself, he owned and tilled considerable land. I de-
tested the trade, preferring almost any other labor; but I was fond
of agriculture, and of all employment in which horses were used.
We had, among other lands, fifty acres of forest within a mile of the
village. In the fall of the year choppers were employed to cut enough
wood to last a twelvemonth.

When I was seven or eight years of age, I began hauling all the
wood used in the house and shops. I could not load on the wagons,
but I could drive, and the choppers would load, and someone at
the house unload. When about eleven years old, I was strong enough
to hold a plow. From that age until seventeen I did all the work
done with horses, such as breaking up the land, furrowing, plowing
corn and potatoes, bringing in the crops when harvested, hauling
all the wood, besides tending two or three horses, a cow or two,
and sawing wood for stoves, while still attending school.

For this I was compensated by the fact that there was never any scolding or punishing by my parents; no objection to rational enjoyments, such as fishing, going to the creek a mile away to swim in summer, taking a horse and visiting my grandparents in the adjoining county fifteen miles off, skating on the ice in winter, or taking a horse and sleigh when there was snow on the ground.

Cincinnati, 1830

While still quite young I had visited Cincinnati, forty-five miles away, several times alone; also Maysville, Kentucky, and once Louisville. The journey to Louisville was a big one for a boy of that day. I had also gone once with a two-horse carriage to Chilicothe, about seventy miles, with a neighbor's family, who were removing to Toledo, Ohio, and returned alone; and had gone once, in like manner, to Flatrock, Kentucky, about seventy miles away. On this latter occasion I was fifteen years of age.

Louisville, 1830

While at Flatrock, at the house of a Mr. Payne, whom I was visiting with his brother, a neighbor of ours in Georgetown, I saw a very fine saddle horse, which I rather coveted, and proposed to Mr. Payne, the owner, to trade him for one of the two I was driving.

Payne hesitated to trade with a boy, but his brother told him that it would be alright, that I was allowed to do as I pleased with the horses. I was seventy miles from home, with a carriage to take back, and Mr. Payne said he did not know that his horse had ever had a collar on. I asked to have him hitched to a farm wagon and we would soon see whether he would work. It was soon evident that the horse had never worn harness before; but he showed no viciousness, and I expressed a confidence that I could manage him.

The fine art of horse trading, 1840

A trade was at once struck, I receiving ten dollars' difference. The next day Mr. Payne and I started on our return. We got along very well for a few miles, until we encountered a ferocious dog that frightened the horses and made them run. The new animal kicked at every jump he made. I got the horses stopped, however, before any damage was done, and without running into anything. After giving them a little rest, to quiet their fears, we started again. That instant the new horse kicked, and started to run once more. The road we were on struck the turnpike within half a mile of the point where the second run-away commenced, and there was an embankment twenty or more feet deep on the opposite side of the pike.

I got the horses stopped on the very brink of the precipice. My new horse was terribly frightened and trembled like an aspen; but he was not half so badly frightened as my companion, Mr. Payne, who deserted me after this last experience, and took passage on a freight wagon for Maysville. Every time I attempted to start, my new horse would commence to kick. I was in quite a dilemma for a time.

Once in Maysville I could borrow a horse from an uncle who lived there; but I was more than a day's travel from that point. Finally I took out my bandana, the style of handkerchief in universal use then, and with this blindfolded my horse. In this way I reached Maysville safely the next day, no doubt much to the surprise of my friend. Here I borrowed a horse from my uncle, and the following day we proceeded on our journey.

Chilton White

About half my school days in Georgetown were spent at the school of John D. White, a North Carolinian, and the father of Chilton White who represented the District in Congress for one term during the Rebellion.

Chilton is reported to have told of an earlier horse-trade of mine. As he told the story, there was a Mr. Ralston living within a few miles of the village, who owned a colt which I very much wanted. My father had offered twenty dollars for it, but Ralston wanted twenty-five. I was so anxious to have the colt, that after the owner left, I begged to be allowed to take him at the price demanded. My father yielded, but said twenty-dollars was all the horse was worth, and told me to offer that price; if it was not accepted I was to offer twenty-two and a half, and if that would not get him, to give the twenty-five.

I at once mounted a horse and went for the colt. When I got to Mr. Ralston's house, I said to him: "Pap says I may offer you twenty dollars for the colt, but if you won't take that, I am to offer twenty-two and a half, and if you won't take that, to give you twenty-five."

It would not require a Connecticut man to guess the price finally agreed upon. This story is nearly true. I certainly showed very plainly that I had come for the colt and meant to have him. I could not have been over eight years old at the time. This transaction caused me great heart-burning. The story got out among the boys of the village, and it was a long time before I heard the last of it.

I kept the horse until he was four years old, when he went blind, and I sold him for twenty dollars. When I went to Maysville to school in 1836, at the age of fourteen, I recognized my colt as one of the blind horses working on the tread-wheel of the ferryboat. I have described enough of my early life to give an impression of the whole. I did not like to work; but I did as much of it while young, as grown men can be hired to do in these days, and attended school at the same time. I had as many privileges as any boy in the village, and probably more than most of them.

But at school the case was different. The rod was freely used there, and I was not exempt from its influence.

West Point on the Hudson River, 1839

CHAPTER II

"To West Point: I Have Applied for It."

IN the winter of 1838–9 I was attending school at Ripley, only ten miles' distance from Georgetown, but spent the Christmas holidays at home. During this vacation my father received a letter from the honorable Thomas Morris, then United States Senator from Ohio. When he read it he said to me, "Ulysses, I believe you are going to receive the appointment." "What appointment?" I inquired. "To West Point; I have applied for it." "But I won't go," I said. He said he thought I would, *and I thought so too if he did!*

[39]

West Point from Old Fort Putnam, 1839

I really had no objection to going to West Point, except that I had a very exalted idea of the acquirements necessary to get through. I did not believe I possessed them, and could not bear the idea of failing. There had been four boys from our village, or its immediate neighborhood, who had been graduated from West Point, and never a failure of anyone appointed from Georgetown, except in the case of the one whose place I was to take. He was the son of Dr. Bailey, our nearest and most intimate neighbor. Young Bailey had been appointed in 1837. Finding before the January examination following, that he could not pass, he resigned and went to a private school, and remained there until the following year when he was re-appointed.

Before the next examination he was dismissed. Dr. Bailey was a proud and sensitive man, and felt the failure of his son so keenly that he forbade his return home. There were no telegraphs in those days to disseminate news rapidly, no railroads west of the Alleghanies, and but few east; and above all, there were no reporters prying into other people's private affairs. Consequently, it did not become generally known that there was a vacancy at West Point from our district until I was appointed.

The Hon. Thomas L. Hamer

The Honorable Thomas L. Hamer was our member of Congress at the time, and had the right of nomination. He and my father had been members of the same debating society (where they were generally pitted on opposite sides), and intimate personal friends from their early manhood up to a few years before.

In politics they differed. Hamer was a life-long Democrat, while my father was a Whig. They had a warm discussion, which finally became angry—over some act of President Jackson; the removal of the deposit of public moneys I think, after which they never spoke until after my appointment.

President Andrew Jackson

Louisville, Kentucky

I knew both of them felt badly over this estrangement, and would have been glad at any time to come to a reconciliation; but neither would make the advance. Under these circumstances my father would not write to Hamer for the appointment, but he wrote to Thomas Morris, United States Senator from Ohio, informing him that there was a vacancy at West Point from our District, and that he would be glad if I could be appointed to fill it. This letter, I presume, was turned over to Mr. Hamer, and, as there was no other applicant, he cheerfully appointed me. This healed the breech between the two, never after reopened.

Philadelphia, 1839

Going to West Point would give me the opportunity of visiting the two great cities of the continent, Philadelphia and New York. This was enough. When these places were visited I would have been glad to have had a steamboat or railroad collision, or any other accident happen, by which I might have received a temporary injury sufficient to make me ineligible to enter the Academy. Nothing of the kind occurred, and I had to face the music.

New York City, 1840

I took passage on a steamer at Ripley, Ohio, for Pittsburg, about the middle of May, 1839. On this occasion we had no vexatious delays, and in about three days Pittsburg was reached. From Pittsburg I chose passage by the canal to Harrisburg, rather than by the more expeditious stage. No mode of conveyance could be more pleasant when time was not an object.

From Harrisburg to Philadelphia there was a railroad, the first I had ever seen, except the one on which I had just crossed the summit of the Alleghany Mountains, and over which canal boats were transported. In travelling by the road from Harrisburg, I thought the perfection of the rapid transit had been reached. We travelled at least eighteen miles an hour when at full speed, and made the whole distance averaging probably as much as twelve miles an hour. This seemed like annihilating space.

Philadelphia

I stopped five days in Philadelphia, saw about every street in the city, attended the theatre, visited Gerard College (which was then in course of construction), and got reprimanded afterwards for dallying by the way so long.

My sojourn in New York was shorter, but long enough to enable me to see the city very well.

New York

West Point, Steamboat Landing

I reported to West Point on the 31st of May, and about two weeks later, passed my examination for admission, without difficulty, very much to my surprise.

Names	Cadets Signature.	Date of Report	Aug 1st July September		Cadets place of residence	
			Yrs	Mos	Town	County
F. M. W. Burton	Frank Stark William Burton	June 3rd	17	8	Murfreesboro	Rutherford
Francis W. Ely Lea x	Francis W. Ells Lea (Register)	Aug 26	18	7	Cleveland	Bradley
R. Hazlett,	Robert Hazlett	June 10	18	5	Warren	Trumbull
U. S. Grant,	Ulysses Hiram Grant	May 25	17	2	Georgetown	Brown
H. F. Reynolds	William Franklin					
Chas. S. Gillispie						

I, Cadet *U. S. Grant*, of the State of *Ohio*, aged *Seventeen* years and *two* months, do hereby engage, with the consent of my guardian, to serve in the Army of the United States for eight years, unless sooner discharged by the proper authority. And I, Cadet *U. S. Grant*, do hereby pledge my word of honor as a gentleman, that I will faithfully observe the Rules and Articles of War, the Regulations for the Military Academy; and that I will in like manner, observe and obey the orders of the President of the United States, and the orders of the officers appointed over me, according to the rules and discipline of War.

Subscribed to at West Point, N.Y., this *14th* day of *September* eighteen hundred and *thirty nine*, in presence of

U. S. Grant

A. S. Grant
Bvt. 2d Lt. 4th Infy.

A military life had no charms for me, and I had not the faintest idea of staying in the army even if I should be graduated, which I did not expect.

The encampment which preceded the commencement of academic studies was very wearisome and uninteresting. When the 28th of August came—the date for breaking up camp and going into barracks—I felt as though I had been at West Point always, and that if I stayed to graduation, I would have to remain always.

Trading with the Indians
an original drawing by Cadet U. S. Grant

I did not take hold of my studies with avidity, in fact I rarely ever read over a lesson the second time during my entire cadetship.

West Point Library, 1838

I could not sit in my room doing nothing. There is a fine library connected with the Academy from which cadets can get books to read in their quarters. I devoted more time to these than to books relating to the course of studies.

Washington Irving

James Fenimore Cooper

Much of the time, I am sorry to say, was devoted to novels, but not those of a trashy sort. I read all of Bulwer's then published, Cooper's, Marryat's, Scott's, Washington Irving's works, Lever's and many others that I do not now remember. Mathematics was very easy to me, so that when January came I passed the examination, taking a good standing in that branch. In French, the only other study at that time in the first year's course, my standing was very low. In fact, if the class had been turned the other end foremost, I should have been near head.

Infantry tactics, West Point Military Academy, 1839

Artillery practice,
West Point Military Academy
1839

I never succeeded in getting squarely at either end of my class in any one study during the four years. I came near it in French, artillery, infantry and cavalry tactics, and conduct.

During my first year's encampment General Scott visited West Point and reviewed the cadets. With his commanding figure, his quite colossal size and showy uniform, I thought him the finest specimen of manhood my eyes had ever beheld, and the most to be envied. I could never resemble him in appearance, but I believe I did have a presentiment for a moment that some day I should occupy his place on review.

The next summer Martin Van Buren, then president of the United States, visited West Point and reviewed the cadets; he did not impress me with the awe which Scott had inspired. In fact, I regarded General Scott and Captain C. F. Smith, commandant of cadets, as the two men most to be envied in the nation. I retained a high regard for both up to the day of their death.

The last two years wore away more rapidly than the first two, but they still seemed to me about five times as long as Ohio years. At last all examinations were passed, and the members of the class were called upon to record their choice of arms of service and regiments. I was anxious to enter the cavalry, or Dragoons as they were then called, but there was only one regiment of dragoons in the army at that time, and attached to that, besides the full compliment of officers, there were brevet second lieutenants. I recorded therefore my first choice, dragoons; second, 4th Infantry; and got the latter.

Soldiers of the United States Army, 1840
Dragoons, Infantry and Artillery

Cadets "Sam" Grant and Alexander Hayes at West Point, 1844
A rare engraving from an original daguerreotype made in 1844, Grant stands on the left, Alexander Hayes, Grant's closest friend, holds the horse's bridle. Hayes, a major general on Grant's staff in 1864, was killed at Spotsylvania Court House.

St. Louis, Missouri, in 1844

CHAPTER III

With a War in Prospect

ON September 30th I reported for duty at Jefferson Barracks, St. Louis, with the 4th United States Infantry. It was the largest military post in the country at the time, being garrisoned by sixteen companies of infantry. Colonel Steven Kearney, one of the ablest officers of the day, commanded the post, and under him, discipline was kept at a high standard, but without vexatious rules or regulations.

Every drill and roll call had to be attended, but in the intervals officers were permitted to enjoy themselves, leaving the garrison and going where they pleased without making written application.

At West Point I had a class-mate—in the last year of our studies —F. T. Dent, whose family resided some five miles West of Jefferson Barracks. Two of his unmarried brothers were living at home at that time and, as I had taken with me from Ohio, my horse, saddle and bridle, I soon found my way out to White Haven, the name of the Dent estate. As I found the family congenial my visits became frequent. There were at home, besides the young men, two daughters, one a school miss of fifteen, the other a girl of eight or nine. There was still an older daughter of seventeen, who had been spending several years at boarding-school in St. Louis, but who, though through school, had not yet returned home.

She was spending the winter in the city with the family of Colonel John O'Fallon, well known in St. Louis. In February she returned to her country home. After that I do not know but my visits became more frequent; they certainly did become more enjoyable. We would often take walks, or go on horse-back to visit the neighbors, until I became quite well acquainted in that vicinity.

If the 4th Infantry had remained at Jefferson Barracks it is possible, even probable, that this life might have continued for some years without my finding out that there was anything serious the matter with me; but in the following May a circumstance occurred which developed my sentiment so palpably that there was no mistaking it.

Julia Dent

President John Tyler

The annexation of Texas was at this time the subject of violent discussion in Congress, in the press, and by individuals. The administration of President Tyler, then in power, was making the most strenuous efforts to effect the annexation, which was, indeed, the great and absorbing question of the day.

Fort Jessup, in Louisiana, 1844

During these discussions the greater part of the single rifle regiment in the Army—the 2nd Dragoons—which had been dismounted a year or two before and designated "Dismounted Rifles," was stationed at Fort Jessup, Louisiana, to go into camp in the neighborhood of Fort Jessup, and there await further orders.

The troops were embarked on steamers and were on their way down the Mississippi within a few days after the receipt of this order.

Steamboat Landing, St. Louis, 1844

About the time they started I obtained a leave of absence for twenty days to go to Ohio to visit my parents. I was obliged to go to St. Louis to take a steamer for Louisville or Cincinnati, or the first steamer going up the Ohio river to any point. Before I left St. Louis orders were received at Jefferson Barracks for the 4th Infantry to follow the 3rd. A messenger was sent after me to stop my leaving; but before he could reach me, I was off, totally ignorant of these events.

My leave of absence required me to report for duty at Jefferson Barracks at the end of twenty days.

Richard Stoddert Ewell, C.S.A.

Accordingly, at the end of the twenty days, I reported for duty to Lieutenant Ewell, commanding at Jefferson Barracks, handing him at that same time my leave of absence. After noticing the phraseology, "at the end of which time he will report for duty with his proper command"—he said he would give me an order to join my regiment in Louisiana. I then asked for a few days' leave before starting, which was readily granted.

This was the same Ewell who acquired a considerable reputation as a Confederate General during the rebellion. He was a man much esteemed, and deservedly so.

The Gravois River

I immediately procured a horse and started for the country, taking no baggage with me, of course. There is an insignificant creek, the Gravois, between Jefferson Barracks and the place to which I was going; not a bridge over it from its source to its mouth. There is not water enough in the creek at ordinary stages to run a coffee mill, and at low water there is none running whatever.

On this occasion it had been raining heavily and, when the creek was reached, I found the banks full to overflowing and the current rapid. I looked at it a moment to consider what to do. One of my superstitions had always been when I started to go anywhere, or to do anything, not to turn back or stop until the thing intended was accomplished. So I struck into the stream, and in an instant the horse was swimming and I being carried down by the current. I headed the horse towards the other bank and soon reached it, wet through and through and without other clothes on that side of the stream. I went on, however, to my destination and borrowed a dry suit from my future brother-in-law.

Jefferson Barracks, St. Louis, Missouri

Before I returned I mustered up courage to make known, in the most awkward manner imaginable, the discovery I had made on learning that the 4th Infantry had been ordered away from Jefferson Barracks. The young lady afterwards admitted that she, too, had experienced a depression of spirits she could not account for when the regiment left. Before separating it was definitely understood that we would join our fortunes. This was in May 1844. It was the 22nd of August, 1848, before the fulfillment of this agreement. My duties kept me on the frontier of Louisiana with the Army of Observation during the dependency of annexation; and afterwards I was absent through the war with Mexico. During that time there was a constant correspondence between Miss Dent and myself, but we only met once in the period of four years and three months.

Colonel Frederick Dent, father of Julia Dent (Grant)

In May, 1845, I procured a leave for twenty days, visited St. Louis, and obtained the consent of the parents for the union, which had not been asked for before.

Albert E. Church, Professor of Mathematics
United States Military Academy

As already stated, it was never my intention to remain in the army long, but to prepare myself for a professorship in some college. Accordingly, soon after I was settled at Jefferson Barracks, I wrote a letter to Professor Church, professor of mathematics at West Point, requesting to ask my designation as his assistant, when next a detail had to be made. Assistant professors at West Point are all officers of the army, supposed to be selected for their special fitness for the particular branch of study they are assigned to teach. The answer from Professor Church was entirely satisfactory, and no doubt I should have been detailed a year or two later, but for the Mexican War coming on.

Camp Salubrity, Louisiana

The 3rd Infantry had selected camping grounds on the reservation at Fort Jessup, about midway between the Red River and the Sabine. Our orders required us to go into camp in the same neighborhood and await further instructions. Those authorized to do so selected a place in the pine woods, between the old town of Natchitoches and Grand Ecore, about three miles from each and on high ground back from the river. The place was given the name of Camp Salubrity and proved entitled to it. The camp was on a high, sandy, pine ridge, with spring branches in the valley in front and rear. The springs furnished an abundance of cool, pure water, and the ridge was above the flight of mosquitoes, which abound in that region in great multitudes and of great voracity. In the valley they swarmed in myriads, but never came to the summit of the ridge.

3rd and 4th Infantry

There was no intimation given that the removal of the 3rd and 4th regiments of infantry to the western border of Louisiana was occasioned in any way by the prospective annexation, but it was generally understood that such was the case. Ostensibly, we were to prevent filibustering into Texas, but really as a menace to Mexico in case she appeared to contemplate war.

William L. Marcy, Secretary of War

In taking military possession of Texas after annexation, the Army of Occupation, under General Taylor, was directed to occupy the disputed territory. The Army did not stop at the Nueces and offered to negotiate for a settlement of the boundary question, but went beyond, apparently in order to force Mexico to initiate war. It is to the credit of the American nation, however, that after conquering Mexico, and while practically holding the country in our possession, so that we could have retained the whole of it, or made any terms we chose, we paid a round sum for the additional territory taken; more than it was worth, or was likely to be, to Mexico. To us it was an empire and of incalculable value; but it might have been obtained by other means.

Fort Jessup, Louisiana

The 4th Infantry went to camp on Salubrity in the month of May, 1844, with instructions to await further orders. At first, officers and men occupied ordinary tents. As the summer heat increased these were covered by sheds to break the rays of the sun.

The Summer was whiled away in social enjoyments among the officers, in visiting those stationed at Fort Jessup, twenty-five miles away;—visiting the planters on the Red River, and the citizens of Natchitoches and Grand Ecore. There was much pleasant intercourse between the inhabitants and the officers of the army. I retained very agreeable recollections of my stay at Camp Salubrity, and of the acquaintances made there, and no doubt my feeling is shared by the few officers living who were there at the time.

New Orleans, Louisiana

Early in July the long expected orders were received, but they only took the regiment to New Orleans Barracks. We reached there before the middle of the month, and again waited weeks for still further orders. The yellow fever was raging in New Orleans during the time we remained there, and the streets of the city had the appearance of a continuous well-observed Sunday.

With a war in prospect, and belonging to a regiment that had an unusual number of officers detailed on special duty away from the regiment, my hopes of being ordered to West Point as instructor vanished.

Corpus Christi, Texas, 1844

CHAPTER IV

The Unholy War

EARLY in September the regiment left New Orleans for Corpus Christi, now in Texas. Ocean steamers were not then common, and the passage was made in sailing vessels. At that time there was not more than three feet of water in the channel at the outlet of Corpus Christi Bay; the debarkation, therefore, had to take place by small steamers, and at an island in the channel called Shell Island, the ships anchoring some miles out from shore. This made the work slow, and as the army was only supplied with one or two steamers, it took a number of days to effect the landing of a single regiment with its stores, camp and garrison equipage.

[75]

Landing of the Naval Expedition on the Tabasco River

There happened to be pleasant weather while this was going on, but the land swell was so great that when the ship and steamer were on opposite sides of the same wave they would be at considerable distance apart. The men and baggage were let down to a point higher than the lower deck of the steamer, and when ship and steamer got into the trough between the waves, and were close together, the load would be drawn over the steamer and rapidly run down until it rested on the deck.

*Mexicans firing on U.S. Naval forces
from the Chapperal. The long boats
in the foreground are being towed.*

Corpus Christi is near the head of the bay of the same name,
formed by the entrance of the Nueces River into tide-water, and
is on the west bank of that bay. At the time of its first occupancy by
United States troops, there was a small Mexican hamlet there, con-
taining probably less than one hundred souls. There was, in addition,
a small American trading post at which goods were sold to Mexican
smugglers.

Corpus Christi army of occupation

Gradually the Army of Occupation assembled at Corpus Christi. When it was all together it consisted of seven companies of the 2nd Regiment of Dragoons, four companies of light artillery, five regiments of infantry, the 3rd, 4th, 5th, 7th and 8th, and one regiment of artillery acting as infantry—not more than 3000 men in all.

General Zachary Taylor commanded the whole

Artilleryman, U.S.A., 1844

There were troops enough in one body to establish a drill and discipline sufficient to fit men and officers for all they were capable of in case of battle.

Infantryman, U.S.A., 1844

Artillery, Infantry and Dragoon officers

Volunteer Infantry

The rank and file were composed of men, who had enlisted in time of peace, to serve for seven dollars a month, and were necessarily inferior as material to the average volunteers enlisted later in the war expressly to fight, and also to the volunteers in the war for the preservation of the Union.

General Quitman

General Worth

The men engaged in the Mexican War were brave, and the officers of the regular army, from highest to lowest, were educated in their profession. A more efficient army, for its number and its armament, I do not believe ever fought a battle than the one commanded by General Taylor in his first two engagements on Mexican or Texan soil.

General Wool

Captain Lee

Valley of Mexico

The presence of United States troops on the edge of the disputed territory furthest from the Mexican settlements, was not sufficient to provoke hostilities. We were sent to provoke a fight, but it was essential that Mexico should commence it. It was very doubtful whether Congress would declare war; but if Mexico should attack our troops, the Executive could announce, "Whereas, war exists by the acts of . . ." and prosecute the contest with vigor. Once initiated there were but few public men who would have the courage to oppose it.

[83]

United States Troops Moving to Matamoros

Mexico showing no willingness to come to the Neuces to drive the invaders from her soil, it became necessary for the "invaders" to approach to within convenient distance to be struck. Accordingly, preparations were begun for moving the army to the Rio Grande, to a point near Matamoros. It was desirable to occupy a position near the largest center of population possible to reach, without absolutely invading territory to which we set up no claim whatever.

The distance from Corpus Christi to Matamoros is one hundred and fifty miles. The country does not abound in fresh water, and the length of the marches had to be regulated by the distance between water supplies. Besides the streams, there were occasional pools, filled during the rainy season, some probably made by the traders who travelled constantly between Corpus Christi and the Rio Grande, and some by the buffalo.

[84]

General Zachary Taylor

General William Twiggs

There was no need for haste, and some months were consumed in the necessary preparations for a move. But at last preparations were complete and orders were issued for the advance to begin on the 8th March. General Taylor had an army of not more than three thousand men. One battery, the siege guns, and all the convalescent troops were sent on by water to Brazos Santiago, at the mouth of the Rio Grande. A guard was left back at Corpus Christi to look after public property and to take care of those who were too sick to be removed. The remainder of the army, probably not more than twenty-five hundred men, was divided into three brigades, with the cavalry independent. Colonel Twiggs, with seven companies of Dragoons and a battery of light artillery, moved on the 8th.

Crossing the Colorado

At the point where the army struck the Colorado River, the stream was quite wide and of sufficient depth for navigation. The water was blackish and the banks were fringed with timber. Here the whole army concentrated before attempting to cross. The army was not accompanied by a pontoon train, and at that time the troops were not instructed in bridge building. To add to the embarrassment of the situation, the army was here, for the first time, threatened with opposition. Buglers, concealed from our view by the brush on the opposite side, sounded the "assembly," and other military calls.

There were probably but few troops, and those engaged principally in watching the movements of the "invader." A few of our cavalry dashed in, forded and swam the stream, and all opposition was soon dispersed. I do not remember that a single shot was fired.

Colorado River, 1844

The troops waded the stream, which was up to their necks in the deepest part. Teams were crossed by packing a long rope to the end of the wagon tongue, passing it between the two swing mules and by the side of the leader, hitching his bridle as well as the bridle of the mules in rear to it, and carrying the end to men on the opposite shore. The bank down to the water was steep on both sides. A rope long enough to cross the river, therefore, was attached to the back axle of the wagon, and men behind would hold the rope to prevent the wagon "beating" the mules into the water. This ladder rope also served the purpose of bringing the end of the forward one back, to be used over again. The water was deep enough for a short distance to swim the little Mexican mules which the army was then using, but they, and the wagons, were pulled through so fast by the men at the end of the rope ahead, that no time was left them to show their obstinacy. In this manner the artillery and transportation of the Army of Occupation crossed the Colorado River.

City of Matamoros

*Public Square,
Matamoros*

About the middle of the month of March the advance of the army reached the Rio Grande and went into camp near the banks of the river, opposite the city of Matamoros, and almost under the guns of a small fort at the lower end of the town.

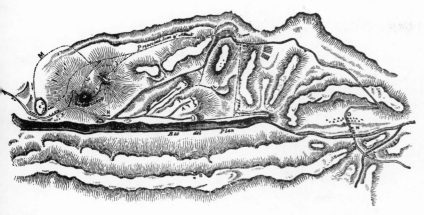

The work of fortifying was commenced at once. The fort was laid out by the engineers, but the work was done by the soldiers under the supervision of their officers, the chief engineer retaining general directions.

The Mexicans now became so incensed at our near approach that some of their troops crossed the river above us, and made it unsafe for small bodies of men to go far beyond the limits of camp.

They captured two companies of Dragoons commanded by Thornton and Hardee. The latter figured as a general in the late war, on the Confederate side, and was author of the tactics first used by both armies.

Point Isabel

There was no base of supplies nearer than Point Isabel, on the coast, north of the mouth of the Rio Grande and twenty-five miles away. The enemy, if the Mexicans could be called such, at this time when no war had been declared, hovered about in such numbers that it was not safe to send a wagon train after supplies with any escort that could be spared.

Mexican Cavalry watching a wagon train

Fort Brown

By the latter part of April the work was in a partially defensible condition, and the 7th Infantry, Major Jacob Brown commanding, was marched in to garrison it with some few pieces of artillery. All the supplies on hand, with the exception of enough to carry the rest of the army at Point Isabel, were left with the garrison, and the march was commenced with the remainder of the command, every wagon being taken with the army.

Walker's Cavalry

*Naval Expedition under Commodore Perry ascending
the Tuspan River preparatory to landing troops.*

Early on the second day after starting the force reached its destination without opposition from the Mexicans. There was some delay in getting supplies ashore from vessels at anchor in the open roadstead.

While General Taylor was away with the bulk of his army, the little garrison up the river was besieged. As we lay in our tents upon the seashore, the artillery at the fort on the Rio Grande could be distinctly heard. The war had begun.

Major Brown mortally wounded

Mexicans

There was no possible means of obtaining news from the garrison, and information from outside could not be otherwise than unfavorable. What General Taylor's feelings were during the suspense I do not know; but for myself, a young second lieutenant who had never heard a hostile gun before, I felt sorry that I had enlisted.

Early in the forenoon of the 8th of May, as Palo Alto was approached, an army, outnumbering our little force, was seen drawn up in line of battle just in front of the timber. Their bayonets and spearheads glistened in the sunlight. The force was composed largely of cavalry armed with lances. Where we were the grass was tall, reaching nearly to the shoulders of the men, and very stiff. Each stock, pointed at the top, was hard and sharp as a darning needle.

Mexican Lancer

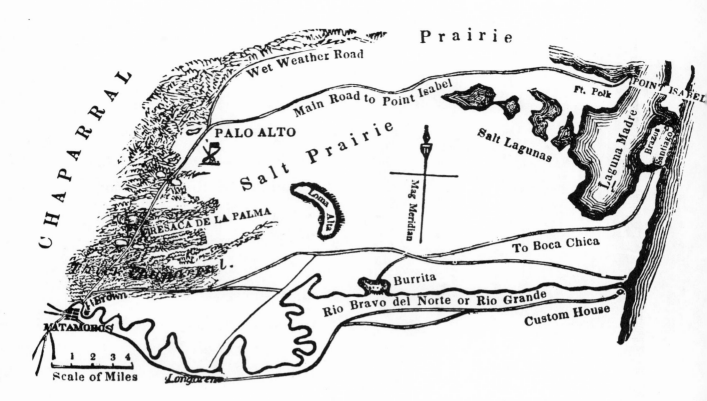

General Taylor halted his army before the head of the column came in range of the Mexican artillery. He then formed a line of battle facing the enemy. His artillery, two batteries and two eighteen pounder iron guns, drawn by oxen, were placed in opposition at intervals along the line. A battalion was thrown to the rear, commanded by Lieutenant-Colonel Childs, of the artillery, as reserve.

These preparations completed, orders were given for a platoon of each company to stack arms and go to a stream off to the right of the command, to fill their canteens and also those of the rest of their respective companies.

Battlegrounds of Palo Alto and Resaca de la Palma

When the men were all back in their places in line, the command to advance was given. As I looked down that long line of about three thousand armed men, advancing towards a larger force also armed, I thought what a fearful responsibility General Taylor must feel commanding such a host and so far away from friends. The Mexicans immediately opened fire on us, first with artillery, and then with infantry.

At first their shots did not reach us, and the advance was continued. As we got nearer, the cannon balls commenced going through the ranks. They hurt no one, however, because they would strike the ground long before they reached our line, and ricochetted through the tall grass so slowly the men would see them and open ranks and let them pass. When we got to a point where the artillery could be used with effect, a halt was called, and the battle opened on both sides.

Mexican Cavalry

During the battle Major Ringgold, an accomplished and brave artillery officer, was mortally wounded, and Lieutenant Luther, also of the artillery, was struck. During the day several advances were made, and just at dusk it became evident that the Mexicans were falling back.

Major Ringgold

May's Charge

We again advanced, and occupied at the close of the battle substantially the ground held by the enemy at the beginning. In this last move there was a brisk fire upon our troops, and some execution was done. One cannon-ball passed through our ranks not far from me. It took off the head of an enlisted man, and the under jaw of Captain Page of my regiment, while the splinters from the musket of the killed soldier, and his brains and bones knocked down two or three others, including one officer, Lieutenant Wallen,—hurting them more or less. Our casualties for the day were nine killed and forty-seven wounded.

Arista's Camp

Rout of the Mexican Cavalry

At the break of day, on the 9th, the army under Taylor was ready to renew the battle; but an advance showed that the enemy had entirely left our front during the night.

There was no further resistance. The evening of the 9th, the army was encamped on its old ground near the fort, and the garrison was relieved. The siege lasted a number of days, but the casualties were few in number. Major Jacob Brown, of the 7th Infantry, the commanding officer, had been killed, and in his honor the fort was named.

The battles of Palo Alto and Resaca de la Palma seemed to us engaged, as pretty important affairs; but we had only a faint conception of their magnitude until they were fought over in the North by the Press and the reports came back to us. At the same time, we learned that war existed between the United States and Mexico, by the acts of the latter country. On learning this fact General Taylor transferred our camps to the south or west bank of the river, and Matamoros was occupied. We then became the "Army of Invasion."

*U.S. Naval Expedition ascending the Tabasco River near
Devil's Bend*

On the 19th of August, the army started for Monterey leaving a
small garrison at Matamoros. The troops, with the exception of the
artillery, cavalry, and the brigade to which I belonged, were moved
up the river to Camargo on steamers.

Those who marched did so by the south side of the river. Lieutenant-Colonel Garland, of the 4th Infantry, commanded the entire
marching force. One day out convinced him that marching by day
in that latitude, in the month of August, was not a beneficial sani-
tary measure, particularly for Northern men. The order of marching
was changed and night marches were substituted with the best
results.

Grand Plaza, Camargo

Camargo, looking north

When Camargo was reached, we found a city of tents outside the Mexican hamlet. I was detailed to act as quartermaster and commissary to the regiment. The teams that had proven abundantly sufficient to transport all supplies from Corpus Christi to the Rio Grande over the level prairies of Texas, were entirely inadequate to the needs of the reinforced army in a mountainous country. To obviate the deficiency, pack mules were hired, with Mexicans to pack and drive them.

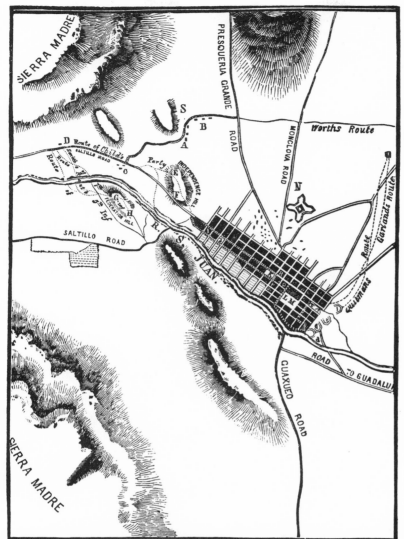

MONTEREY AND ITS APPROACHES.

REFERENCES.

A. Mexican Ambuscade afternoon 20th September.
B. Yard into which Mexicans fired on evening 20th.
C. Charge of Mexican Lancers morning 21st.
D. Position of 2d Division on 21st.
E. Height stormed by Colonel Childs 22d.
F. Bishop's Palace carried on 22d.
G. Height stormed by Captain Smith's Party 21st.
H. Redoubt stormed by General Smith 21st.
I. Arista's House and Garden
J. Church Cemetery, with loop-holes for musketry.
K. Plaza de Carne.
L. Small Plaza.
M. Grand Plaza.
P. Q. R. Positions occupied by our troops morning 24th.
1. Redoubt four guns carried morning 21st.
2. Redoubt Fort Diablo three guns.
6. Redoubt four guns.

Monterey

On the 19th, General Taylor, with his army, was encamped at Walnut Springs, within three miles of Monterey. The town is on a small stream coming out of the mountain pass, and is backed by a range of hills of moderate elevation. To the north, between the city and Walnut Springs, stretches an extensive plain. On this plain, and entirely outside the last houses of the city, stood a strong fort, enclosed on all sides, to which our army gave the name of "Black Fort."

Monterey

The Bishop's Palace

Its guns commanded the approaches to the city to the full extent of their range. There were two detached spurs of hills or mountains to the north and northwest of the city which were also fortified.

On one of these stood the Bishop's Palace. The road to Saltillo leaves the upper or western end of the city under the fire of the guns from these heights. The lower or eastern end was defended by two or three small detached works, armed with artillery and infantry.

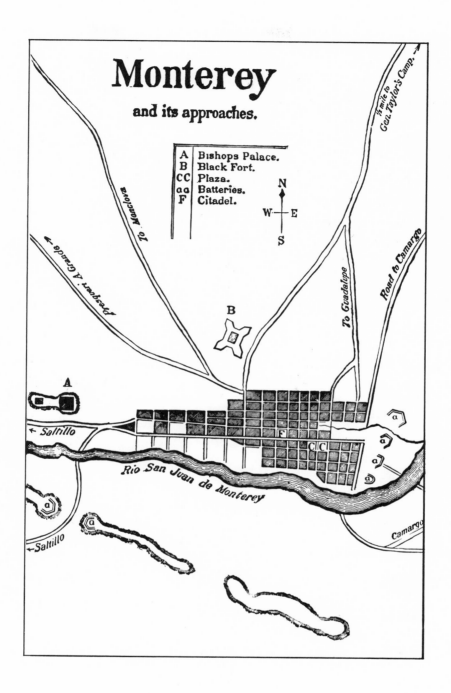

Monterey and its approaches.

A	Bishops Palace.
B	Black Fort.
CC	Plaza.
a a	Batteries.
F	Citadel.

The plaza in the center of the city was the citadel. All the streets leading from it were swept by artillery entrenched behind temporary parapets. The housetops near the plaza were converted into infantry fortifications by the use of sand-bags for parapets. Such were the defenses of Monterey in September, 1847.

General Ampudia, with a force of ten thousand men, was in command. General Taylor's force was about six thousand five hundred strong in three divisions under Generals Butler, Twiggs and Worth. The troops went into camp at Walnut Springs, while the engineer officers, under Major Mansfield, commenced their reconnaissance. Mansfield found that it would be practicable to get troops around to the Saltillo Road, out of range of the "Black Fort" and the works on the detached hills to the northwest of the city. With this road in our possession the enemy would be cut off from receiving further supplies, if not from all communication with the interior.

During the night of the 20th, General Taylor established a battery, consisting of two twenty-four pounder howitzers and a ten-inch mortar, at a point from which they could play upon "Black Fort." A natural depression in the plain, sufficiently deep to protect men standing in it from the fire from the fort, was selected and the battery established on the crest nearest the enemy.

The point for establishing the siege battery was reached and the work performed without attracting the attention of the enemy. At daylight the next morning fire was opened on both sides and continued with, what seemed to me at that day, great fury. My curiosity got the better of my judgement, and I mounted a horse and rode to the front to see what was going on. I had been there but a short time when an order to charge was given, and lacking the moral courage to return to camp, I charged with the regiment.

General Worth, his division somewhat reinforced, was given the task of possession of the Saltillo Road, and of carrying the detached works outside the city.

Monterey, Mexico

By a movement by the left flank, Garland could have led his men beyond the range of the fire from "Black Fort" and advanced toward the northeast angle of the city, as well covered from fire as could be expected. There was no undue loss of life in reaching the lower end of Monterey except that sustained by Garland's command.

Saltillo, Mexico

On the west, General Worth reached the Saltillo Road after some fighting but without heavy loss. He turned from his new position and captured the forts on both heights in that quarter. This gave him possession of the upper or west end of Monterey. Twiggs' and Butler's divisions were in possession of the east end of the town, but the "Black Fort," north of the town, and the Plaza in the center were still in the possession of the enemy.

Meanwhile Quitman's brigade, conducted by an officer of engineers, reached the eastern end of the city, and was placed under cover of the houses without much loss. Colonel Garland's brigade also arrived at the suburbs and, by the assistance of some of our troops that had reached house-tops from which they could fire into a little battery covering the approaches to the lower end of the enemy. An entrance into the east end of the city was now secured, and the houses protected our troops so long as they were inactive.

Twiggs' division was at the lower end of the city and well covered from the fire of the enemy. But the streets leading to the Plaza were commanded from all directions by artillery. The houses were flat-roofed and but one or two stories high. The roofs about the plaza were manned with infantry, the troops protected from our fire by parapets made of sandbags. All advances into the city were thus attended with much danger. While moving along streets which did not lead to the plaza, our men were protected from the fire, and from the view of the enemy except at the crossings; but at these a volley of musketry and a discharge of grape-shot were invariably encountered.

General Zachary Taylor at the Battle of Monterey

When within a square of the plaza this small command, ten companies in all, was brought to a halt. Placing themselves under cover from the shots of the enemy, the men would watch to detect a head above the sand-bags on the neighboring houses. The exposure of a single head would bring a volley from our soldiers.

Military Plaza of San Antonio, as it looked about the time of the Mexican War.

A rare daguerreotype. General Wool and Staff
entering Monterey, Mexico, Calle Real to South, 1847.

We had not occupied this position long when it was discovered that our ammunition was growing low. I volunteered to go back to the point we had started from, report our position to General Twiggs, and ask for ammunition to be forwarded. We were at this time occupying ground off from the street, in rear of the houses. My ride back was an exposed one. Before starting I adjusted myself on the side of my horse furthest from the enemy, and with only one foot holding to the cantle of the saddle, and an arm over the neck of the horse exposed, I started at full run. It was only at street crossings that my horse was under fire, but these I crossed at such a flying rate that generally I was passed and under cover of the next block of houses before the enemy fired. I got out safely without a scratch.

El Paso in 1846

While this was going on at the east, General Worth, with a small division of troops, advancing towards the plaza from the opposite end of the city, resorted to a better expedient for getting to the plaza. Instead of moving by the open streets, he advanced through the houses, cutting passage ways from one to another without much loss of life. He got so near the plaza during the night that before morning Ampudia, the Mexican commander, made overtures for the surrender of the city and garrison. This stopped all further hostilities. The terms of surrender were soon agreed upon.

Mexicans

After the surrender of the garrison of Monterey, a quiet camp life was led until midwinter. As had been the case on the Rio Grande, the people who remained at their homes fraternized with the "Yankees" in the pleasantest manner. In fact, under the humane policy of our commander, I question whether the great majority of the Mexican people did not regret our departure as much as they had regretted our coming.

A Caballero

A Mexican Gentleman

Mexican Guerillas

Peons

General Winfield Scott

When General Scott assumed command of the "Army of Invasion," I was in the division of General David Twiggs, in Taylor's command, but under the new orders my regiment was transferred to the division of General William Worth, in which I served to the close of the war.

General Scott reached Brazos Santiago, at the mouth of the Rio Grande, late in December, 1846, and proceeded at once up the river to Camargo, where he had written General Taylor to meet him. Taylor, however, had gone to Tampico, for the purpose of establishing a post there. He had started on this march before he was aware of General Scott being in the country. Under these circumstances Scott had to issue his orders designating the troops to be withdrawn from Taylor, without the personal consultation he had expected with his subordinate.

[112]

Battle of Buena Vista, February 22, 23, 24, 1847

General Taylor's victory at Buena Vista, February 22nd, 23rd and 24th, 1847, with an army almost entirely composed of volunteers who had not been in battle before, and over a vastly superior force numerically, made his nomination for the Presidency by the Whigs a foregone conclusion.

The troops withdrawn from Taylor, to form part of the forces to operate against Vera Cruz, were assembled at the mouth of the Rio Grande preparatory to embarkation for their destination.

Troop transports, mouth of the Rio Grande, south of Vera Cruz

The army lay in camp upon the sand-beach in the neighborhood of the mouth of the Rio Grande for several weeks, awaiting the arrival of transports to carry it to its new field of operations. The transports were all sailing vessels. The passage was a tedious one, and many of the troops were on shipboard over thirty days from the embarkation at the mouth of the Rio Grande to the time of debarkation south of Vera Cruz.

Finally, on the 7th of March, 1847, the little army of ten or twelve thousand men, given Scott to invade a country with a population of seven or eight millions, a mountainous country affording the greatest possible natural advantages for defense, was all assembled and ready to commence the perilous task of landing from vessels lying in the open sea.

U.S. frigates "Scorpion," "Spitfire," "Vixen," and "Scourge," landing troops, Vera Cruz

The transports with troops were assembled in the harbor of Anton Lizardo, some sixteen miles south of Vera Cruz, as they arrived, and there awaited the remainder of the fleet, bringing artillery, ammunition and supplies of all kinds from the North.

On the 9th of March the troops were landed and the investment of Vera Cruz, from the Gulf of Mexico south of the city to the Gulf again on the North, was soon and easily effected.

Vera Cruz was a walled city. The wall extended from the water's edge south of the town to the water again to the north with fortifications at intervals along the line and at the angles. In front of the city, and on an island half a mile out in the Gulf, stands San Juan de Ulloa, an enclosed fortification of large dimensions and great strength.

[115]

Battle for Vera Cruz, Mexico, March 27, 1847

The siege continued with brisk firing on our side till the 27th of March, by which time a considerable breach had been made in the wall surrounding the city. Upon this General Morales, Governor of both the city and of San Juan De Ulloa, commenced a correspondence with General Scott looking to the surrender of the town, forts and garrisons.

On the 29th, Vera Cruz and San Juan de Ulloa were occupied by Scott's Army. About five thousand prisoners and four hundred pieces of artillery, besides large amounts of small arms and ammunition, fell into the hands of the victorious force. The casualties on our side during the siege amounted to sixty-four officers and men, killed and wounded.

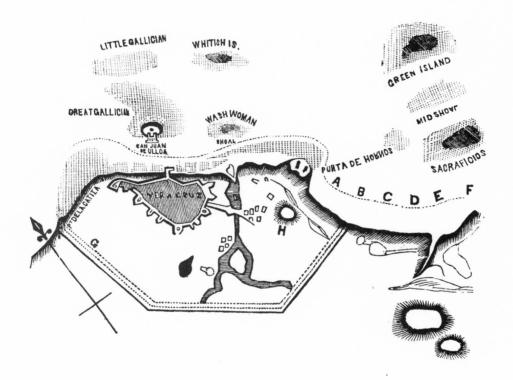

References:

A and C. Positions of the steamers "Spitfire" and "Vixen." G.
American line of entrenchments, established March 13th, extending from Point de la Catita to a point opposite B, B, D,
E, F. The positions of the gunboats. H. A Mexican redoubt
captured by American forces. The sloop of war "John Adams"
was anchored on the South Side of Sacrificios, opposite F.

On the 8th of April, Twiggs' division started for Jalapa, followed very soon by Patterson with his division. Worth was to bring up the rear with his command as soon as transportation enough was assembled. It was the 13th of April before this division left Vera Cruz.

The leading division ran against the enemy at Cerro Gordo, some fifty miles west, on the road to Jalapa, and went into camp at Plan del Rio, about three miles from the fortifications.

Cerro Gordo is one of the highest spurs of the mountains some twelve to fifteen miles east of Jalapa, and Santa Anna had selected this point as the easiest to defend against an invading army. The road, said to have been built by Cortez, zigzags around the mountain side and was defended at every turn by artillery. On either side were deep chasms or mountain walls. A direct attack along the road was an impossibility.

General Scott, at Vera Cruz on the 12th, learning the situation on the front, hastened on to take personal supervision, and at once commenced preparations for the capture of the position held by Santa Anna.

A flank movement seemed equally impossible. After the arrival of the commanding general upon the scene, reconnaissances were sent out to find, or to make, a road by which the rear of the enemy's works might be reached without a frontal attack.

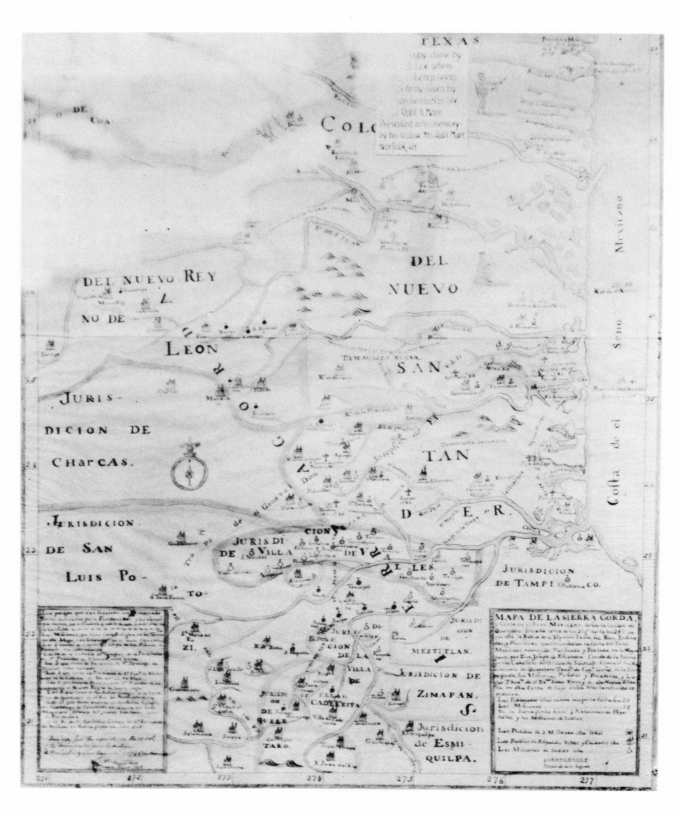

Military Map of Cerro Gordo
made by Captain of Engineers Robert E. Lee

The reconnaissances were made under the supervision of Captain Robert E. Lee, Lieutenants P. T. G. Beauregard, Isaac Stevens, Z. B. Tower, G. W. Smith, George B. McClellan, and J. G. Foster, of the corps of engineers, officers who retained rank and fame on one side or the other in the great conflicts for the preservation of the Union.

This was accomplished by the 17th without the knowledge of Santa Anna or his army. On the same day General Scott issued his orders for the attack on the 18th.

The attack was made as ordered, and perhaps there was not a battle of the Mexican War, or any other, where orders issued before an engagement were nearer being a correct report of what afterwards took place. Under the supervision of the engineers, roadways had been opened over chasms to the right where the walls were so steep that men could barely climb them. Animals could not.

These had been opened under cover of night without attracting the notice of the enemy. The engineers, who had directed the opening, led the way and the troops followed. Artillery was let down the steep slopes by hand, the men engaged attaching a strong rope to the rear axle and letting the guns down a piece at a time, while the men at the ropes kept their ground on top, paying out gradually, while a few at the front directed the course of the piece. The surprise of the enemy was complete. The victory overwhelming. Some three thousand prisoners fell into Scott's hands, also a large amount of ordnance and stores.

Lieutenant P. T. G. Beauregard

Lieutenant Isaac Stevens

Lieutenant G. B. McClellan

Captain R. E. Lee

U.S. Forces marching in detour around Lake Chalco

The route followed by the army from Puebla to the City of Mexico was over Rio Frio Mountain, the road about eleven thousand feet above tide water. The pass through this mountain might have been easily defended, but it was not, and the advance division reached the summit in three days after leaving Puebla.

The City of Mexico lies west of Rio Frio Mountain on a plain backed by another mountain six miles farther west, with others still nearer on the north and south.

Between the western base of Rio Frio and the City of Mexico there are three lakes, Chalco and Xochimilco on the left, and Texcoco on the right, extending to the east end of the City of Mexico. Scott's army was rapidly concentrated about Ayotla and other points near the eastern end of Lake Chalco.

Battle of Valencia Contreras

General Scott at once set his engineers reconnoitering the works about Contreras, and on the 19th movements were commenced to get troops into positions from which an assault could be made. This affair, like that of Cerro Gordo, was an engagement in which the officers of the engineer corps won special distinction.

Contreras is situated on the south of a mountain, near its face, where volcanic rocks are piled in great confusion reaching nearly to San Antonio. This made the approach to the city very difficult.

The enemy outside the city outnumbered our soldiery three to one, but they had become so demoralized by the succession of defeats this day, that the City of Mexico could have been entered without much further bloodshed.

Battle of Churubusco

Churubusco proved to be about the severest battle fought in the Valley of Mexico. General Scott, coming upon the battlefield about this juncture, ordered two brigades under Shields to move north and turn the right of the enemy. This Shields did, but not without hard fighting and heavy loss. The enemy finally gave way, leaving in our hands prisoners, artillery and small arms.

Captain Philip Kearney, afterwards a general in the war of the rebellion, rode with a squadron of cavalry to the very gates of the city, and would, no doubt, have entered with his little force, only at that point he was badly wounded, as were several of his officers. He had not heard the call for a halt.

General Franklin Pierce

General Franklin Pierce had joined the army in Mexico, at Puebla, a short time before the advance upon the capital commenced. He had subsequently not been in any of the engagements of the war up to the battle of Contreras. By an unfortunate fall of his horse on the afternoon of the 19th, he was painfully injured.

Captain Philip Kearney

General Winfield Scott

General Santa Anna

The army took positions along the slope of the mountains south of the city as far west as Tacubaya. Negotiations were at once entered into with Santa Anna, who was then practically "the Government," and the immediate commander. A truce was signed which denied to either party the right to strengthen its position or to receive reinforcements.

The Mexicans felt so outraged at the terms that they commenced preparations for defense, without giving notice of the termination of the armistice.

The news reached General Scott of the violation of the armistice about the 4th of September. He wrote a vigorous letter to President Santa Anna, calling his attention to it and, receiving an unsatisfactory reply, declared the armistice at an end.

General Scott, with Worth's division, was occupying Tacubaya, a village some four miles south west of the City of Mexico, extending from the base up to the mountain side for the distance of half a mile. More than a mile west, and also a little above the plain, stands Molino del Rey, a long stone structure, one story high and several hundred feet in length.

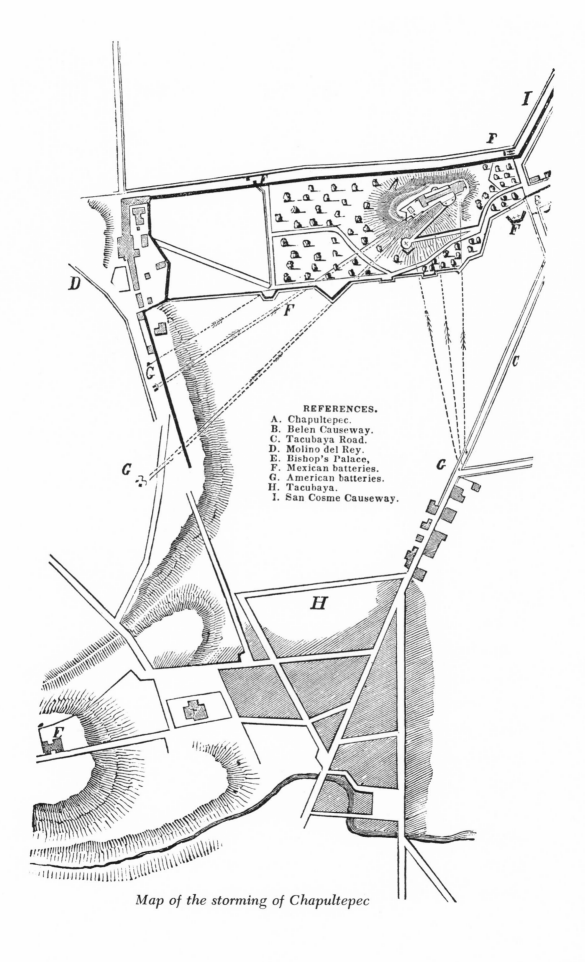

REFERENCES.
A. Chapultepec.
B. Belen Causeway.
C. Tacubaya Road.
D. Molino del Rey.
E. Bishop's Palace,
F. Mexican batteries.
G. American batteries.
H. Tacubaya.
I. San Cosme Causeway.

Map of the storming of Chapultepec

North side, Garita de Belen

The City of Mexico is supplied with water by two aqueducts, resting on strong stone arches. One of these aqueducts draws its supply of water from a mountain stream coming into it at or near Molino del Rey, and runs north close to the west base of Chapultepec; thence along the center of a wide road, until it reaches the road running east to the city by the Garita San Cosme. The aqueduct and road both run east to the city. The second aqueduct starts from the east base of Chapultepec, where it is fed by a spring, and runs northeast to the city.

Chapultepec is a mount springing up from the plain to the height of probably three hundred feet, in a direct line between Molino del Rey and the western part of the city. It was fortified both on the top and on the rocky and precipitous sides.

San Cosme Gate and Aqueduct

This aqueduct, like the other, runs in the middle of a broad road-way, thus leaving a space on each side. The arches supporting the aqueducts afford a protection for advancing troops as well as to those engaged defensively.

At points on the San Cosme road parapets were thrown across, with an embrasure for a single piece of artillery in each. At the point where both road and aqueduct turn at right angles, from north to east, there was not only one of these parapets supplied by one gun and infantry supports, but the houses to the north of the San Cosme road, facing south and commanding a view of the road back to Chapultepec, were covered with infantry, protected by parapets made of sandbags.

Battle of Molino del Rey

The battle of Molino del Rey was fought on the 8th of September. By daylight the troops to be engaged at Molino were all at the places designated. The engagement did not last many minutes, but the killed and wounded were numerous for the number of troops engaged.

During the night of the 11th, batteries were established which could play upon the fortifications of Chapultepec. The bombardment commenced early on the morning of the 12th, but there was no further engagement during this day than that of the artillery. General Scott assigned the capture to General Pillow, but did not leave the details to his judgment. Two assaulting columns, two hundred and fifty men each, composed of volunteers, were formed. They were commanded by Captains McKinzie and Casey respectively. The assault was successful, but bloody.

General Pillow's troops advancing through the woods to attack Chapultepec

The roads leading to the Garitas (the gates) San Cosme and Belen, by which these aqueducts enter the city, were strongly entrenched. Deep, wide ditches filled with water lined the sides of both roads. Such were the defenses of the City of Mexico in September, 1847, on the routes over which General Scott entered.

Garita de Belen, south side

Battle of Chapultepec, September 13, 14, 1847

Mexico City, 1847

The night of September 13th was spent by the troops under General Worth, in the houses near San Cosme, and in line confronting the general line of the enemy across to Belen. The troops that I was with were in the houses north of the road leading into the city, and were engaged during the night in cutting passage-ways from one house to another towards the town. During the night Santa Anna, with his army, except the deserters, left the city.

General Scott soon followed the troops into the city, in state. He took quarters at first in the "Halls of the Montezumas," and from there issued his wise and discreet orders for the Government of a conquered city.

Washington, D.C., 1848

CHAPTER V

Flush Times and Private Life

THE treaty of peace between the two countries was signed by the commissioners of each side early in February, 1848. It took considerable time for it to reach Washington, receive the approval of the administration, and be fully ratified by the Senate.

My experience in the Mexican War was of great advantage to me afterwards. Besides the many practical lessons it taught, it brought nearly all the officers of the regular army together so as to make them personally acquainted. It also brought them in contact with the volunteers, many of whom served in the war of the rebellion afterwards.

General Robert E. Lee, C.S.A., Commander of the
Army of Northern Virginia

The acquaintance thus formed was of immense service to me in the war of the rebellion. I mean what I learned of the characters of those to whom I was afterwards opposed. I do not pretend to say that all movements, or even many of them, were made with special reference to the characteristics of the commander against whom they were directed. But my appreciation of my enemies was certainly affected by this knowledge.

The natural disposition of most people is to clothe a commander of a large army whom they do not know, with almost superhuman abilities. A large part of the National army, for instance, and most of the press of the country, clothed General Lee with just such qualities, but I had known him personally, and knew that he was mortal; and it was just as well that I felt this.

James Knox Polk, eleventh President of the United States
1845–1849

The treaty of peace was at last ratified and the evacuation of Mexico of United States troops was ordered. Early in June the troops in the City of Mexico began to move out. My regiment was sent to Pascagoula, Mississippi, to spend the summer. As soon as it was settled in camp I obtained a leave of absence for four months and proceeded to St. Louis.

Julia Dent Grant

On the 22nd of August, 1848, I was married to Miss Julia Dent, the lady of whom I have before spoken. We visited my parents and relations in Ohio and, at the end of my leave, proceeded to my post at Sackett's Harbor, New York.

Sackett's Harbor, New York, 1848

Senator Zachariah Chandler of Michigan

In April following I was ordered to Detroit, Michigan, where two years were spent with but few important incidents. The present constitution of the State of Michigan was ratified during this time. By the terms of one of its provisions, all citizens of the United States residing within the State at the time of the ratification became citizens of Michigan also. During my stay in Detroit there was an election of city officers. Mr. Zachariah Chandler was the candidate of the Whigs for the office of mayor, and was elected, although the city was then reckoned Democratic. This was Mr. Chandler's first entry into politics, a career he followed ever after with great success, and in which he died enjoying the friendship, esteem and love of his countrymen.

U.S. Army Post, Governors Island, New York, 1851

In the Spring of 1851 the garrison at Detroit was transferred to Sackett's Harbor, and in the following Spring the entire 4th Infantry was ordered to the Pacific Coast. It was decided that Mrs. Grant should visit my parents at first for a few months, and then remain with her own family at their St. Louis home until an opportunity offered of sending for her.

In the month of April the regiment was assembled at Governors Island, New York Harbor, and, on the 5th of July, eight companies sailed for Aspinwall. We numbered a little over seven hundred persons, including the families of officers and soldiers.

Aspinwall, Isthmus of Panama, 1852

In eight days Aspinwall was reached. At that time the streets of the town were eight to ten inches under water, and foot passengers passed from place to place on raised foot walks. July is at the height of the wet season on the Isthmus. At intervals rain would pour down in streams, followed in not many minutes by a blazing, tropical summer sun.

These alternate changes from rain to sunshine, were continuous in the afternoons. I wondered how any person could live many months in Aspinwall, and wondered still more why anyone tried.

Terminus of the Panama Railroad, Isthmus of Panama, 1852

In the summer of 1852, the Panama Railroad was completed only to the point where it now crosses the Chagres River. From there passengers were carried by boats to Gorgona, at which place they took mules for Panama, some twenty-five miles further. Those who travelled over the Isthmus in those days will remember that boats on the Chagres River were propelled by natives not inconveniently burdened with clothing. These boats carried thirty to forty passengers each. The crews consisted of six men to a boat, armed with long poles. There were planks wide enough for a man to walk on conveniently, running along the sides of each boat from end to end. The men would start from the bow, place one end of their poles against the river bottom, brace their shoulders against the other end, and then walk to the stern as rapidly as they could. In this way from a mile to a mile and a half an hour could be made against the current of the river.

Chagres River, Isthmus of Panama, 1852

The regiment, with the exception of one company left as guards to the public property, camp and garrison equipage principally, and the soldiers with families, took boats, propelled as above described, for Gorgona. From this place they marched to Panama, and were soon comfortably on the steamer anchored in the bay, some three or four miles from the town.

I, with one company of troops and all the soldiers with families, all the tents, mess chests and camp kettles, was sent to Cruces, a town a few miles higher up the Chagres River than Gorgona. There I found an impecunious American who had taken the contract to furnish transportation for the regiment at a stipulated price per hundred pounds for the freight and so much for each saddle animal. But when we reached Cruces there was not a mule, either for pack or saddle, in the place.

San Francisco, 1852. Ships, abandoned by their crews, beached and converted into stores and hotels to ease the building shortage

Meanwhile the cholera had broken out, and men were dying every hour. To diminish the food for the disease, I permitted the Company detailed with me to proceed to Panama. The Captain and the doctors accompanied the men, and I was left alone with the sick and the soldiers who had families.

I was about a week at Cruces before transportation began to come in. About one-third of the people with me died, either at Cruces or on the way to Panama. There was no agent of the transportation company at Cruces to consult, or to take the responsibility of procuring transportation at a price which would secure it. I therefore dismissed the contractor and made a new contract with a native, at more than double the original price. Thus we finally reached Panama.

By the last of August the cholera had so abated that it was deemed safe to start. The disease did not break out again on the way to California, and we reached San Francisco early in September.

San Francisco Post Office, 1852

San Francisco at that day was a lively place. Gold, or placer dig-
gings, as it was called, was at its height. Steamers plied daily between San Francisco and both Stockton and Sacramento. Passengers
and gold from the southern mines came by the Stockton boats; from
the northern mines by Sacramento.

A San Francisco gambling saloon

Long Wharf, San Francisco, 1852

In the evening when these boats arrived, Long Wharf—there was but one wharf in San Francisco in 1852—was alive with people crowding to meet the miners as they came down to sell their "dust" and to "have a time."

Those early days in California brought out character. It was a long way off then, and the journey was expensive. The fortunate could go by Cape Horn, or by the Isthmus of Panama; but the mass of pioneers crossed the plains with their ox-teams. This took an entire summer. They were very lucky when they got through with a yoke of worn-out cattle. The immigrant, on arriving, found himself a stranger in a strange land far from friends.

My regiment spent a few weeks at Benicia Barracks, and then was ordered to Fort Vancouver, on the Columbia River, then in Oregon Territory. During the winter of 1852–3, the Territory was divided, all north of the Columbia River being taken from Oregon to make Washington Territory.

Fort Vancouver, Washington Territory, 1852–53

While I was stationed on the Pacific Coast we were free from Indian Wars. There were quite a number of remnants of tribes in the vicinity of Portland, in Oregon, and of Fort Vancouver, in Washington Territory. They had generally acquired some of the vices of civilization, but none of the virtues, except in individual cases. The Hudson Bay Company had held the Northwest with their trading posts for many years before the United States was represented on the Pacific Coast. They still retained posts along the Columbia River and one at Fort Vancouver, when I was there. Their treatment of the Indians had brought out the better qualities of the savages.

During my years on the Columbia River, the smallpox exterminated one small remnant of a band of Indians entirely, and reduced others materially. I do not think there was a case of recovery among them, until the doctor with the Hudson Bay Company took the matter in hand and established a hospital. Nearly every case he treated recovered.

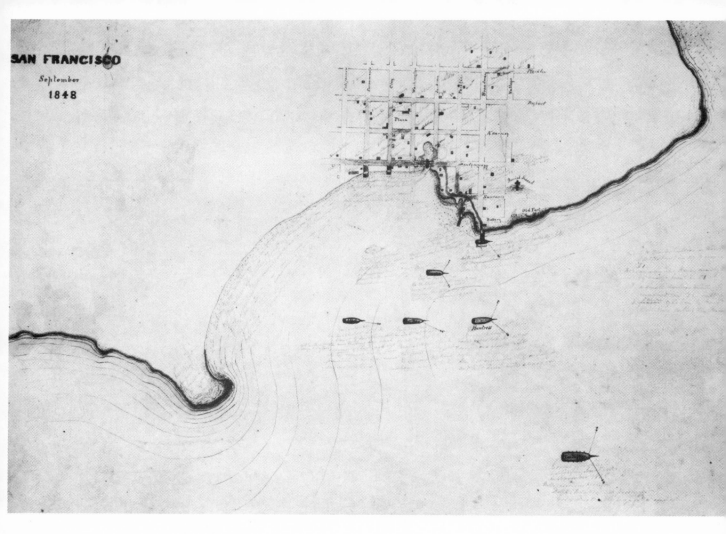

San Francisco

The death of Colonel Bliss, of the Adjutant General's Department, which occurred July 5th, 1853, promoted me to the captaincy of a company then stationed at Humboldt Bay, California. The notice reached me in September of the same year, and I very soon started to join my new command.

I was obliged to remain in San Francisco for several days before I found a vessel. This gave me a good opportunity of comparing the San Francisco of 1852 with that of 1853. In 1853 the town had grown out into the bay beyond what was the end of the Long Wharf when I first saw it. Streets and houses had been built out on piles where the year before the largest vessels visiting the port lay at anchor or tied to the Wharf.

San Francisco, 1853

There was no filling under the streets or houses. San Francisco presented the same general appearance as the year before; that is, eating, drinking and gambling houses were conspicuous for their number and publicity. They were on the first floor, with doors wide open. At all hours of the day and night in walking the streets, the eye was regaled, on every block near the waterfront, by the sight of players at faro. Often broken places were found in the street, large enough to let a man down into the water below. I have but little doubt that many of the people who went to the Pacific Coast in the early days of the gold excitement, and have never been heard from since, or who were heard from for a time and ceased to write, found watery graves beneath the houses or streets built over San Francisco Bay.

Julia Dent Grant, daughter Nellie, Colonel Frederick Dent,
Mrs. Grant's father, Frederick Dent Grant, Jr.

My family, all this while, was at the East. It consisted now of a wife and two children. I saw no chance of supporting them on the Pacific Coast out of my pay as an army officer. I concluded, therefore, to resign, and in March applied for leave of absence until the end of the July following, tendering my resignation to take effect at the end of that time.

I left the Pacific Coast very much attached to it, and with the full expectation of making it my future home. That expectation and that hope remained uppermost in my mind until the Lieutenant-Generalcy Bill was introduced into Congress in the winter of 1863—4. The passage of that bill, and my promotion, blasted my last hope of ever becoming a citizen of the further West.

St. Louis, 1854

PART TWO

CHAPTER VI

The Coming Crisis

IN the late summer of 1854 I rejoined my family, to find in it a son whom I had never seen, born while I was on the Isthmus of Panama. I was now to commence, at the age of thirty-two, a new struggle for our support. My wife had a farm near St. Louis, to which we went, but I had no means to stock it. A house had to be built also. I worked very hard, never losing a day because of bad weather, and accomplished the object in a moderate way. If nothing else could be done I would load a cord of wood on a wagon and take it to the city for sale. I managed to keep along very well until 1858, when I was attacked by fever and ague. I had suffered very severely and for a long time from this disease, while a boy in Ohio. It lasted now over a year and, while it did not keep me in the house, it did interfere greatly with the amount of work I was able to perform.

Mrs. Julia Dent Grant with son Frederick and daughter, Nellie

In the winter I established a partnership with Harry Boggs, a cousin of Mrs. Grant, in the Real Estate agency business. I spent that winter at St. Louis myself, but did not take my family into town until the Spring. Our business might have become prosperous if I had been able to wait for it to grow. As it was, there was no more than one person could attend to, and not enough to support two families.

While a citizen of St. Louis and engaged in the real estate agency business, I was a candidate for the office of county engineer, an office of respectability and emolument which would have been very acceptable to me at that time. The encumbent was appointed by the county court, which consisted of five members. My opponent had the advantage of birth over me (he was a citizen by adoption) and carried off the prize.

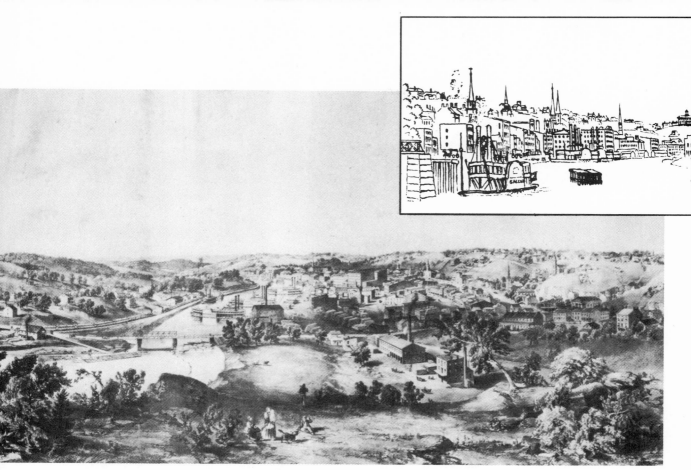

Galena, Illinois, 1860

I now withdrew from the co-partnership with Boggs and, in May, 1860, removed to Galena, Illinois, and took a clerkship in my father's store.

Grant and Perkins' Store, Galena, Illinois, 1865

Henry Clay, leader of the Whig Party

While a citizen of Missouri, my first opportunity for casting a vote at a Presidential election occurred. I had been in the army from before attaining my majority and had thought but little about politics, although I was a Whig by education and a great admirer of Mr. Clay. But the Whig Party had ceased to exist before I had an opportunity of exercising the privilege of casting a ballot; the Know-Nothing Party had taken its place, but was on the wane; and the Republican Party was in a chaotic state, and had not yet received a name. It had no existence in the Slave States except at points on the borders next to Free States.

Southerners lynching a Northern Abolitionist agitator in Kentucky

As the time for the Presidential election of 1856, the first at which I had the opportunity of voting, approached, party feelings began to run high. The Republican Party was regarded in the South and the border States, not only as opposed to the extension of slavery, but as favoring the compulsory abolition of the institution without compensation to the owners.

Treason to the Government was openly advocated and was not rebuked. It was evident to my mind that the election of a Republican President in 1856 meant the secession of all the Slave States and rebellion.

[155]

James Buchanan, President of the United States, 1856–1860

Under these circumstances I preferred the success of a candidate whose election would prevent or postpone secession, to seeing the country plunged into a war the end of which no man could tell. With a Democrat elected by the unanimous vote of the Slave States, there could be no pretext for secession for four years. I very much hoped that the passion of the people would subside in that time and the catastrophe be averted altogether; if it was not, I believed the country would be better prepared to receive the shock and to resist it. I therefore voted for James Buchanan for President.

Senator Stephen Arnold Douglas of Illinois

During the eleven months that I lived in Galena prior to the first call for volunteers, I had been strictly attentive to my business, and had made but few acquaintances other than customers and people engaged in the same line with myself. When the election took place in November, 1860, I had not been a resident of Illinois long enough to gain citizenship and could not, therefore, vote.

I was really glad of this at the time, for my pledges would have compelled me to vote for Stephen A. Douglas, who had no possible chance of election.

John Cabell Breckenridge   *Abraham Lincoln of Illinois*

The contest was really between Mr. Breckenridge and Mr. Lincoln; between minority rule and rule by the majority.

I wanted, as between these candidates, to see Mr. Lincoln elected.

Excitement ran high during the canvass, and torch-light processions enlivened the scene in the generally quiet streets of Galena many nights during the campaign.

President-Elect Abraham Lincoln poses for his first official photograph for Mathew Brady, February 27th, 1861

The Republican candidate was elected, and solid substantial people of the Northwest, and I presume the same order of people throughout the entire North, felt very serious, but determined after this event. It was very much discussed whether the South would carry out its threat to secede and set up a separate government, the cornerstone of which should be, protection to the "Divine" institution of slavery.

Senator Jefferson Davis of Mississippi, 1861

Fort Sumter, Charleston Harbor, S. C., April 14th, 1861.

CHAPTER VII

A Shot Fired at Fort Sumter

THE winter of 1860–61 will be remembered by middle-aged people of today as one of great excitement. South Carolina promptly seceded after the result of the Presidential election was known. Other Southern States proposed to follow. In some of them the Union sentiment was so strong that it had to be suppressed by force.

Meanwhile the Administration of President Buchanan looked helplessly on and proclaimed that the general government had no power to interfere; that the Nation had no power to save its own life. Mr. Buchanan had in his Cabinet two members at least, who were as earnest—to use a mild term—in the Cause of Secession as Mr. Davis or any Southern statesman.

John Buchanan Floyd

One of them, Floyd, Secretary of War, scattered the army so that much of it could be captured when hostilities should commence, and distributed the cannon and small arms from Northern arsenals throughout the South so as to be on hand when treason wanted them.

Inauguration of Jefferson Davis as President of the Southern Confederacy, Montgomery, Alabama, 1861.

The Navy was scattered in like manner. The President did not prevent his Cabinet preparing for war upon their Government, either by destroying its resources or storing them in the South until a *de facto* government was established with Jefferson Davis as its President, at Montgomery, Alabama, as the Capitol.

But the harm had already been done.

The 4th of March, 1861, came, and Abraham Lincoln was sworn to maintain the Union against all its enemies. The secession of one State after another followed, until eleven had gone out. On the 11th of April, Fort Sumter, a National fort in the harbor of Charleston, South Carolina, was fired upon by the Southerners and a few days after was captured.

Fort Sumter, Charleston Harbor, S.C., 1861

Major Robert Anderson, Commandant of Fort Sumter, surrendered the fort to General P. T. G. Beauregard after a bloodless battle of thirty-four hours, April 14th, 1861.

Upon the firing on Sumter President Lincoln issued his first call for troops and soon after a proclamation convening Congress in extra session. The call was for seventy-five thousand volunteers for ninety days' service.

As soon as the news of the call for volunteers reached Galena, posters were stuck up calling for a meeting of the citizens at the courthouse in the evening. Business ceased entirely; all was excitement; for a time there were no party distinctions; all were Union men, determined to avenge the insult to the National flag.

Governor Yates of Illinois

Up to that time I do not think I had been introduced to Governor Yates or had even spoken to him. I knew him by sight, however, because he was living at the same hotel and I often saw him at table. The evening I was to quit the Capital, I left the supper room before the Governor and was standing at the front door when he came out. He spoke to me, calling me by my old army title, "captain," and said he understood that I was about to leave the city. I answered that I was. He said he would be glad if I would remain over-night and call at the Executive office the next morning.

I complied with his request, and was asked to go into the Adjutant-General's office and render such assistance as I could, the Governor saying that my army experience would be of great service there. I accepted the proposition.

Major General George Brinton McClellan, U.S.A.

Having but little to do after the muster of the last of the regiments authorized by the State legislature, I asked and obtained of the Governor leave of absence for a week to visit my parents in Covington, Kentucky, immediately opposite Cincinnati. General McClellan had been made a Major General and had his headquarters at Cincinnati.

In reality, I wanted to see him. I had known him slightly at West Point, where we served one year together, and in the Mexican War. I was in hopes that when he saw me he would offer me a position on his staff. I called on two successive days at his office, but failed to see him on either occasion and returned to Springfield.

Recruiting Volunteers

While I was absent from the State Capital on this occasion the President's second call for troops was issued. This time it was for 300,000 men for three years or the war. This brought into the United States' service all the regiments then in the State service.

The 21st Regiment of Infantry, mustered in by me at Mattoon, refused to go into the service with the colonel of their selection in any position. While I was still absent Governor Yates appointed me colonel of this latter regiment. A few days after, I was in charge of it and in camp on the Fair Grounds near Springfield.

Brigadier General Ulysses S. Grant

I had not been in Mexico (Missouri) many weeks when, reading a St. Louis paper, I found the President had asked the Illinois Delegation in Congress to recommend some citizens of the State for the position of Brigadier-General, and that they had unanimously recommended me as first on a list of seven. I was very much surprised because my acquaintance with the congressmen was very limited, and I did not know of anything I had done to inspire such confidence.

The papers of the next day announced that my name, with three others, had been sent to the Senate, and a few days after our confirmation was announced.

*Cape Girardeau, Missouri, Important Strategic Position
on the Mississippi between Cairo and St. Louis.*

Troops had been ordered from Ironton to Cape Girardeau, sixty or seventy miles to the southeast, on the Mississippi River; while the forces at Cape Girardeau had been ordered to move to Jacksonville, ten miles out toward Ironton; and troops at Cairo and Bird's Point, at the junction of the Ohio and Mississippi Rivers, were to hold themselves in readiness to go down the Mississippi to Belmont, eighteen miles below, to be moved west from there when an officer should come to command them. I was the officer who had been selected for this purpose. Cairo was to be my headquarters when the expedition terminated.

Union Troops Embarking, Cairo, Illinois, 1861

CHAPTER VIII

From Belmont to Shiloh

THE day after I assumed command at Cairo a man came to me who said he was a scout of General Fremont. He reported that he had just come from Columbus, a point on the Mississippi, twenty miles below on the Kentucky side, and that troops had started from there, or were about to start, to seize Paducah, at the mouth of the Tennessee. There was no time for delay; I reported by telegraph to the department commander the information I had received, and added that I was taking steps to get off that night to be in advance of the enemy in securing that important point.

There was a large number of steamers lying at Cairo, and a good many boatmen were staying in the town. It was the work of only a few hours to get the boats manned, with coal aboard and steam up.

Arrival of General Frémont's Division at Jefferson City,
capital of Missouri, October, 1861

In the latter part of October General Fremont took the field in person and moved from Jefferson City against General Sterling Price, who was then in the State of Missouri with a considerable command.

General John C. Frémont

Embarking Union troops, Fort Holt, opposite Cairo, Illinois, 1861

I dispatched Colonel Oglesby at once with troops sufficient to compete with the reported number of the enemy.

Troops were also designated to go aboard. The distance from Cairo to Paducah is about forty-five miles. I did not wish to get there before daylight of the 6th, and directed therefore that the boats should lie at anchor out in the stream until the time to start.

Not having received an answer to my first dispatch, I again telegraphed to department headquarters that I should start for Paducah that night unless I received further orders.

Then I gathered up all the troops at Cairo and Fort Holt, except suitable guards, and moved them down the river on steamers convoyed by two gunboats accompanying them myself.

[173]

General Grant's army aboard steamers heading down the

We dropped down the river on the 6th to within about six miles of Columbus, debarked a few men on the Kentucky side and established pickets to connect with the troops from Paducah.

My force consisted of a little over three thousand men, and embraced five regiments of infantry, two guns and two companies of cavalry.

Mississippi River for Belmont, Missouri, November 6th, 1861

About two o'clock on the morning of the 7th, I learned that the enemy was crossing troops from Columbus to the west bank to be dispatched, presumably, after Oglesby. I knew there was a small camp of Confederates at Belmont, immediately opposite Columbus, and I speedily resolved to push down the river, land on the Missouri side, capture Belmont, break up the camp and return.

[175]

Battle of Belmont, Missouri, opposite Columbus, Kentucky,
November 7th, 1861. Federal Forces, General U. S. Grant.

By this time the enemy discovered that we were moving upon
Belmont and sent out troops to meet us. Soon after we had started
in line, his skirmishers were encountered and fighting commenced.
This continued, growing fiercer and fiercer for about four hours,
the enemy being forced back gradually until driven into his camp.

Confederates Forces, Major General Leonidas Polk.

The ground on the west shore of the river, opposite Columbus, is low, and in places, marshy and cut up with sloughs. The soil is rich and the timber large and heavy. There were some small clearings between Belmont and the point where we landed, but most of the country was covered with the native forests. We landed in front of a cornfield.

[177]

General U. S. Grant in 1861

The two objects for which the battle of Belmont was fought were fully accomplished. The enemy gave up all idea of detaching troops from Columbus. His losses were heavy for that period of the war. Belmont was severely criticised in the North as a wholly unnecessary battle, barren of results, or the possibility of them from the beginning.

If it had not been fought, Colonel Oglesby would probably have been captured or destroyed with his three thousand men. Then I should have been culpable indeed.

Battle of Mill Springs (Logan's Crossroads), Kentucky, between the forces of Brigadier General George H. Thomas, U.S.A., and Major General George B. Crittenden, C.S.A., January 19th, 1862

From the battle of Belmont until early in February, 1862, the troops under my command did little except prepare for the long struggle which proved to be before them. The enemy at this time occupied a line running from the Mississippi River at Columbus to Bowling Green and Mill Springs, Kentucky. Each of these positions was strongly fortified, as were also points on the Tennessee and Cumberland rivers near the Tennessee State line.

The works on the Tennessee were called Fort Heiman and Fort Henry, and that on the Cumberland was Fort Donelson. At these points the two rivers approached within eleven miles of each other. The lines of rifle pits at each place extended back from the water at least two miles, so that the garrisons were in reality only seven miles apart. These positions were of immense importance to the enemy; and of course correspondingly important for us to possess ourselves of.

On the 1st of February I received full instructions from department headquarters to move upon Fort Henry. On the 2nd the expedition started.

Fort Donelson was the gate to Nashville, a place of great military and political importance, and to a rich country extending far east in Kentucky.

Fort Henry occupies a bend in the river which gave the guns in the water battery a direct fire down the stream.

The camp outside the fort was intrenched, with rifle pits and outworks two miles back on the road to Donelson and Dover. The garrison of the fort and camp was about 2,800, with strong reinforcements from Donelson halted some miles out. There were seventeen heavy guns in the fort. The river was very high, the banks being overflowed except where the bluffs came to the water's edge.

Bombardment of Fort Henry by the Mississippi Flotilla, February 6th, 1862. The gunboats, after a severe shelling of an hour and a half, captured the fort. (General Lloyd Tilghman and staff were captured.)

At the hour designated the troops and gunboats started. General Smith found Fort Heiman had been evacuated before his men arrived. The gunboats soon engaged the water batteries at very close quarters, but the troops which were to invest Fort Henry were delayed for want of roads, as well as by the dense forest and the high water, in what would in dry weather have been unimportant beds of streams.

This delay made no difference in the result. On our first appearance Tilghman had sent his entire command, with the exception of about one hundred men left to man the guns in the fort, to the outworks on the road to Dover and Donelson, so as to have them out of range of the guns of our navy; and before any attack on the 6th he had ordered them to retreat on Donelson.

Attack on Fort Donelson. Charge of the 8th Missouri and 11th Indiana Zouaves, February 15th, 1862. General Lew Wallace, whose troops were comparatively fresh, made the assault. By 5 p.m. the enemy disappeared from the field

The distance from Fort Henry to Donelson is but eleven miles. Prompt action on our part was imperative.

I was very impatient to get to Fort Donelson because I knew the importance of the place to the enemy and supposed he would reinforce it rapidly. I started from Fort Henry with 15,000 men, including eight batteries and part of a regiment of cavalry and, meeting with no obstruction to detain us, the advance arrived in front of the enemy by noon.

The conditions for battle were much more favorable to us than they had been for the first two days of the investment. From the 12th to the 14th we had but 15,000 men of all arms, and no gunboats. Now we had been reinforced by a fleet of six naval vessels, a large division of troops under General L. Wallace.

The plan was for the troops to hold the enemy within his lines, while the gunboats should attack the water batteries at close quarters and silence his guns if possible.

Battle of Fort Donelson at its height, February 15th, 1862

Just as I landed I met Captain Hillyer of my staff, white with fear, not for his personal safety, but for the safety of the National troops.

The enemy had come out in full force to cut his way out and make his escape. McClernand's division had to bear the brunt of the attack from this combined force. His men had stood up gallantly until the ammunition in their cartridge boxes gave out. There was abundance of ammunition nearby lying on the ground in boxes.

We rode rapidly to Smith's headquarters, where I explained the situation to him and directed him to charge the enemy's works with his whole division, saying at the same time that he would find nothing but a very thin line to contend with.

The outer line of rifle pits was passed, and the night of the 15th General Smith, with much of his division, bivouacked within the lines of the enemy. There was no doubt but that the Confederates must surrender or be captured the next day.

Scene of the surrender of Fort Donelson

General Simon Bolivar Buckner

Grant's famous "unconditional surrender" terms and Buckner's capitulation

Headquarters Army in the Field,
Camp Near Donelson, February 16th, 1862
General S. B. Buckner, Confederate Army.
Confederate Army
Sir:

Yours of this date proposing armistice and appointment of Commissioners to settle terms of capitulation, is just received. No terms except an unconditional and immediate surrender can be accepted. I propose to move immediately upon your works. I am, sir,

Very respectfully,
Your ob't se'v't,
U.S. Grant,
Brig. Gen.

Headquarters, Dover, Tennessee,
February 16, 1862.
To Brig. Gen'l. U. S. Grant,
U.S. Army.
Sir:

The distribution of the forces under my command, incident to an unexpected change of commanders, and the overwhelming force under your command, compel me, notwithstanding the brilliant success of the Confederate arms yesterday, to accept the ungenerous and unchivalrous terms which you propose. I am, sir,

Your very ob't se'v't
S. B. Buckner, Brig. Gen. C.S.A.

Major General Ulysses S. Grant

The news of the fall of Fort Donelson caused great delight all over the North. At the South, particularly in Richmond, the effect was correspondingly depressing. I was promptly promoted to the grade of Major General of Volunteers, and confirmed by the Senate. All three of my division commanders were promoted to the same grade, and the colonels who commanded brigades were made brigadier generals in the volunteer service.

I at once put all the troops at Savannah in motion for Pittsburg Landing, knowing that the enemy was fortifying at Corinth and collecting an army there under Johnston.

Some two or three miles from Pittsburg Landing was a log meeting-house called Shiloh. It stood on the ridge which divides the waters of Snake and Lick Creeks,

Battle of Shiloh Church, or Pittsburg Landing
April 6th and 7th, 1862

The position of our troops made a continuous line from Lick Creek on the left to Owl Creek, a branch of Snake Creek, on the right, facing nearly south and possibly a little west. The water in all these streams was very high at the time and contributed to protect our flanks.

The enemy was compelled therefore to attack directly in front. This he did with great vigor, inflicting heavy losses on the National side, but suffering much heavier on his own.

In a very short time the battle became general all along the line. This day everything was favorable to the Union side. We had now become the attacking party. The enemy was driven back all day, as we had been the day before, until finally he beat a precipitate retreat.

[186]

Skirmishing in the advance on Vicksburg

CHAPTER IX

Vicksburg

VICKSBURG was important to the enemy because it occupied the first high ground coming close to the river below Memphis. From there a railroad runs east, connecting with other roads leading to all points of the Southern States. A railroad also starts from the opposite side of the river, extending west as far as Shreveport, Louisiana.

Vicksburg was the only channel connecting the parts of the Confederacy divided by the Mississippi. So long as it was held by the enemy, free navigation of the river was prevented. Hence its importance.

Points on the river between Vicksburg and Port Hudson were held as dependencies; but their fall was sure to follow the capture of the former place.

Major General U. S. Grant as he looked before Vicksburg

The campaign against Vicksburg commenced on the 2nd of November as indicated in a dispatch to the General-in-Chief in the following words:

"I have commenced a movement on Grand Junction, with three divisions from Corinth and two from Bolivar. Will leave here [Jackson, Tennessee] tomorrow, and take command in person. If found practicable, I will go to Holly Springs, and, maybe, Grenada, completing railroad and telegraph as I go."

Union soldiers of the Western Armies, 1862–63.

Lieutenant General John B. Pemberton, C.S.A.,
Defender of Vicksburg

Major Gen. John B. McClernand, U.S.A.

On the 20th, General Van Dorn appeared at Holly Springs, my secondary base of supplies, captured the garrison of 1,500 men commanded by Colonel Murphy, of the 8th Wisconsin Regiment, and destroyed all our munitions, food and forage. The capture was a disgraceful one to the officer commanding.

This interruption in my communications north—I was really cut off from communication with a great part of my own command during this time—resulted in Sherman's moving from Memphis before McClernand could arrive, for my dispatch of the 18th did not reach McClernand. Pemberton got back to Vicksburg before Sherman got there.

Troops of the Western Army, 21st Michigan Infantry, U.S.A.

The rebel positions were on a bluff on the Yazoo River, some miles above its mouth. The waters were high so that the bottoms were generally overflowed, leaving only narrow causeways for dry land between points of debarkation and the high bluffs. These were fortified and defended at all points.

The winter of 1862–63 was a noted one for continuous water in the Mississippi and for heavy rains along the lower river. To get dry land, or rather land above the water to encamp the troops upon, took many miles of river front. We had to occupy the levees and the ground immediately behind.

This was so limited that one corps, the 17th, under General McPherson, was at Lake Providence, seventy miles above Vicksburg.

It was in January the troops took their positions opposite Vicksburg. The water was very high and the rains were incessant. There seemed no possibility of a land movement before the end of March or later, and it would not do to lie idle all this time. The effect would be demoralizing to the troops and injurious to their health.

Vicksburg, Mississippi, at the time of its investment, 1863

Vicksburg is built on this highland. The Mississippi washes the base of the hill. Haine's Bluff, eleven miles from Vicksburg, on the Yazoo River, was strongly fortified. The whole distance from there to Vicksburg and thence to Warrenton was also intrenched, with batteries at suitable distances and rifle pits connecting them.

Champion's Hill where Pemberton had chosen his position to receive us, whether taken by accident or design, was well selected. It is one of the highest points in that section and commanded all the ground in range. On the east side of the ridge, which is quite precipitous, is a ravine running first north, then westerly, terminating at Baker's Creek. It was grown thickly with large trees and undergrowth.

Battle of Champion's Hill. Pemberton's first attempt to halt Grant's advance on Vicksburg, May 16th, 1863.

The battle of Champion's Hill lasted about four hours, hard fighting, preceded by two or three hours of skirmishing, some of which almost rose to the dignity of battle. Every man of Hovey's division and of McPherson's two divisions was engaged during the battle.

We had in this battle about 15,000 men absolutely engaged. Our loss was 410 killed, 1,844 wounded and 187 missing.

I now determined on a second assault. Johnston was in my rear, only fifty miles away, with an army not much inferior in numbers to the one I had with me.

Grant's final attack on Vicksburg, May 22nd, 1863

The attack was ordered to commence on all parts of the line at 10 o'clock A.M. on the 22nd of May, with a furious cannonade from every battery in position.

The attack was gallant, and portions of each of the three corps succeeded in getting up to the very parapets of the enemy and in planting their battle flags upon them; but at no place were we able to enter; and thus ended the last assault upon Vicksburg.

I now determined upon a regular siege—"to outcamp the enemy," as it were, and to incur no more losses. My line was more than fifteen miles long, extending from Haine's Bluff to Vicksburg, thence to Warrenton. The line of the enemy was about seven.

On July 3rd about 10 o'clock A.M., white flags appeared on a portion of the rebel works. Hostilities along that part of the line ceased at once.

Upper left: Grant receives Pemberton's first message. Above: Grant and Pemberton meet at the stone house. Lower left: Grant arriving at Pemberton's headquarters.

At 3 o'clock Pemberton appeared at the point suggested in my verbal message, accompanied by the same officers who had borne his letter of the morning. Our place of meeting was on a hillside within a few hundred feet of the rebel lines. Nearby stood a stunted oak tree, which was made historical by the event. It was but a short time before the last vestige of its body, root and limb, had disappeared, the fragments taken as trophies. Since then the same tree has furnished as many cords of wood, in the shape of trophies, as the "True Cross."

I rode into Vicksburg with the troops, and went to the river to exchange congratulations with the navy upon our joint victory. This news, with the victory at Gettysburg won the same day, lifted a great load of anxiety from the minds of the President, his Cabinet and the loyal people all over the North. The fate of the Confederacy was sealed when Vicksburg fell.

Major General U. S. Grant

Although Grant wears the stars of a major general in this photograph, it is an excellent likeness of the Union Army's most successful commander. Interestingly enough, Master Frederick Dent Grant, the general's young son, accompanied him on this campaign. He can be seen talking to Assistant Secretary of War Charles Dana in the drawing in the upper left corner of the preceding page.

Battle of Murfreesboro (Stone's River), December 31, 1862–January 3, 1863

Battle of Chickamauga, September 19–20, 1863

Battle of Lookout Mountain, November 24, 1863

Officers of Grant's Command at Lookout Mountain photographed after the battle

Above: Union Army military bridge into Chattanooga. Lookout Mountain appears in the distance. Below: Grant as he appeared shortly before his call to Washington to receive his commission of Lieutenant General of the Armies of the United States.

The Executive Mansion in 1863

PART THREE

CHAPTER X

Lieutenant General Grant

THE bill restoring the grade of lieutenant general of the army had passed through Congress and became a law on the 26th of February 1864.

My nomination had been sent to the Senate on the 1st of March and confirmed the next day. I was ordered to Washington on the 3rd to receive my commission, and started the day following that.

The commission was handed to me on the 9th. It was delivered to me at the Executive Mansion by President Lincoln in the presence of his Cabinet, my eldest son, those of my staff who were with me, and a few other visitors.

The President in presenting my commission read from a paper—stating, however, as a preliminary and prior to the delivery of it, that he had drawn that up on paper, knowing my disinclination to speak in public, and handed me a copy in advance so that I might prepare a few lines of reply.

The President said:

"General Grant, the nation's appreciation of what you have done and its reliance upon you for what remains to be done in the existing great struggle, are now presented, with this commission, constituting you lieutenant general in the Army of the United States. With this high honor, devolves upon you, also, a corresponding responsibility. As the country herein trusts you, so, under God, it will sustain you. I scarcely need to add, that, with what I here speak for the nation, goes my own hearty personal concurrence."

To this I replied:

"Mr. President, I accept the commission, with gratitude for the high honor conferred. With the aid of the noble armies that have fought in so many fields for our common country, it will be my earnest endeavor not to disappoint your expectations. I feel the full weight of the responsibilities now devolving on me; and I know that if they are met, it will be due to those armies, and above all, to the favor of that Providence which leads both nations and men."

Major General James B. McPherson, U.S.A.

Major General William T. Sherman, U.S.A.

Major General G. Gordon Meade, U.S.A.

Major General John A. Logan, U.S.A.

It had been my intention before this to remain in the West, even if I was made lieutenant general; but when I got to Washington and saw the situation it was plain that here was the point for the commanding general to be. No one else could, probably, resist the pressure that would be brought to bear upon him to desist from his own plans and pursue others.

I determined therefore, before I started back, to have Sherman advanced to my late position, McPherson to Sherman's in command of the department, and Logan to the command of McPherson's corps. These changes were all made on my recommendation and without hesitation.

Edwin McMasters Stanton, Secretary of War   *Major General Henry W. Halleck, U.S.A.,*
Chief of Staff

Assuring him that I would do the best I could with the means at hand, and avoid as far as possible annoying him or the War Department, our first interview ended.

I did not communicate my plans to the President, nor did I to the Secretary of War or to General Halleck.

March 26th my headquarters were at Culpeper, Virginia, and the work of preparing for an early campaign commenced.

Grant's troops drilling before the Wilderness, April, 1864

In the East, the opposing forces stood in substantially the same relations towards each other as three years before, or when the war began; they were both between the Federal and Confederate capitals.

The Union armies were now divided into nineteen departments, though four of them in the West had been concentrated into a single military division. The Army of the Potomac was a separate command and had no territorial limits.

Before this time these various armies had acted separately and independently of each other, giving the enemy an opportunity often of depleting one command, not pressed, to reinforce another more actively engaged. I determined to stop this.

General R. E. Lee

General Sherman at Chattanooga

Major General Joseph E. Johnston

My general plan now was to concentrate all the force possible against the Confederate Armies in the field. There were but two such as we have seen, east of the Mississippi River and facing north. The Army of Northern Virginia, General Robert E. Lee commanding, was on the south bank of the Rapidan, confronting the Army of the Potomac; the second, under General Joseph E. Johnston, was at Dalton, Georgia, opposed to Sherman who was still at Chattanooga.

Besides these main armies the Confederates had to guard the Shenandoah Valley, a great storehouse to feed their armies from, and their line of communications from Richmond to Tennessee. Accordingly I arranged for a simultaneous movement all along the line.

[205]

General Philip Henry Sheridan and Staff. Left to right: standing, Generals H. E. Davis, Philip Sheridan, Alfred Torbert. Seated: Generals David McMurtrie Gregg, Wesley Merritt, James Harrison Wilson.

In one of my early interviews with the President I expressed my dissatisfaction with the little that had been accomplished by the cavalry so far in the war. I said I wanted the very best man in the army for that command. Halleck was present and spoke up, saying: "How would Sheridan do?" I replied: "The very man I want." The President said I could have anybody I wanted. Sheridan was telegraphed for that day, and on his arrival was assigned to the command of the cavalry corps with the Army of the Potomac.

General Grant's favorite horse, "Cincinnati."

CHAPTER XI

Armageddon: 1864

SOON after midnight, May 3rd–4th, the Army of the Potomac moved out from its position north of the Rapidan, to start upon that memorable campaign destined to result in the capture of the Confederate capital and the army defending it.

This was not to be accomplished, however, without as desperate fighting as the world has ever witnessed; not to be consummated in a day, a week, a month, or a single season.

Ten days' rations, with a supply of forage and ammunition, were taken in wagons. Beef cattle were driven with the trains, and butchered as wanted. Three days' rations in addition, in haversacks, and fifty rounds of cartridges, were carried on the person of each soldier.

Grant's Council of War, Massaponax Church, Virginia, May 21st, 1864. General Grant is seated on the bench, smoking a cigar, with his back to the smaller tree. General George G. Meade, Commander of the Army of the Potomac, is seated on the bench farther left, reading a map. May 21st, 1864.

The country roads were narrow and poor. Most of the country is covered with a dense forest, in places, like the wilderness along the Chickahominy, almost impenetrable even for infantry except along the roads. All bridges were naturally destroyed before the National troops came to them.

The battlefield from the crossing of the Rapidan until the final movement from the wilderness towards Spottsylvania was of the same character. There were some clearings and small farms within what might be termed the battlefield; but generally the country was covered with a dense forest. The roads were narrow and bad. All the conditions were favorable for defensive operations.

*Pontoon bridges over the Rapidan at Germanna Ford, May 4th,
1864*

As soon as the crossing of the infantry was assured, the cavalry pushed forward, Wilson's division by Wilderness Tavern to Parker's Store, on the Orange Plank Road; Gregg to the left towards Chancellorsville. Warren followed Wilson and reached the Wilderness Tavern by noon, took position there and intrenched. Sedgewick followed Warren. He was across the river and in camp on the south bank, on the right of Warren, by sundown. Hancock, with the 2nd Corps, moved parallel with Warren and camped about six miles east of him.

Before night all the troops, and by the evening of the 5th, the trains of more than four thousand wagons, were safely on the south side of the river.

Above: General Robert E. Lee, Commander of the Army of Northern Virginia. Above, left: Lieutenant General James Longstreet. Lower, left: Lieutenant General Ambrose Powell Hill.

On discovering the advance of the Army of the Potomac, Lee ordered Hill, Ewell and Longstreet, each commanding corps, to move to the right to attack us, Hill on the Orange Plank Road, Longstreet to follow on the same road. Longstreet was at this time—middle of the afternoon—at Gordonsville, twenty or more miles away. Ewell was ordered by the Orange Pike. He was nearby and arrived some four miles east of Mine Run before bivouacking for the night.

At six o'clock, before reaching Parker's Store, Warren discovered the enemy. He sent word back to this effect, and was ordered to halt and prepare to meet and attack him.

Major General Winfield Scott Hancock and Staff.
Left to right: Generals Francis C. Barlow, Han-
cock, David Birney and John Gibbon.

Major General Ambrose E. Burnside

Burnside moved promptly on the 4th, on receiving word that the Army of the Potomac had safely crossed the Rapidan. By making a night march of forty miles to reach the river, he was crossing the head of his column early on the morning of the 5th.

The ground fought over had varied in width, but averaged three-quarters of a mile. The killed, and many of the severely wounded, of both armies, lay within this belt where it was impossible to reach them.

Hancock moved by the left of the Orange Plank Road, and Wadsworth by the right of it. The fighting was desperate for about an hour when the enemy began to break up in great confusion. At 4:15 in the afternoon Lee attacked our left. His line moved up to within a hundred yards of ours and opened a heavy fire.

Fighting between Hancock and Hill continued until night put a close to it. Neither side made any special progress.

Battle of the Wilderness, May 5th and 6th, 1864

This status was maintained for about half an hour.

The woods were set on fire by the bursting shells, and the conflagration raged. The wounded who had not the strength to move themselves were either suffocated or burned to death. But the battle still raged, our men firing through the flames until it became too hot to remain longer.

Lee was now in distress. His men were in confusion, and his personal efforts failed to restore order. During the night all Lee's army withdrew within their fortifications. This ended the Battle of the Wilderness.

Burying the dead of the Battle of the Wilderness, May 5th and 6th, 1864

Major General Ben Butler and Staff, Bermuda Hundred, Virginia, 1864. Butler, the officer seated wearing carpet slippers, was trapped with his Army of the James at Bermuda Hundred by General P. T. G. Beauregard. 1864.

My object in moving to Spottsylvania was twofold. First, I did not want Lee to get back to Richmond in time to attempt to crush Butler before I could get there. Second, I wanted to get between his army and Richmond if possible and, if not, to draw him into the open field. But Lee, by accident, beat us to Spottsylvania.

The Mattapony River is formed by the junction of the Mat, the Ta, the Po and the Ny rivers, the last being the northernmost of the four. It takes its rise about a mile south and a little east of Wilderness Tavern. The Po rises southwest of the same place, but farther away. Spottsylvania is on the ridge dividing these two streams, where they are but a few miles apart.

*Battle of Spotsylvania Courthouse, Virginia, second major battle
in the Wilderness campaign. May 8–21, 1864.*

The Brock Road reaches Spottsylvania without crossing either of
these streams. Lee's Army, coming up by the Catharpin Road, had
to cross the Po at Wooden Bridge. Warren and Hancock came by
the Brock Road.

Sedgewick crossed the Ny at Catharpin Furnace. Burnside, coming by Aldriches to Gate's House, had to cross the Ny near the
enemy. He found pickets at the bridge, but they were soon driven
off by a brigade of Wilcox's division, and the stream was crossed.
This brigade was furiously attacked; but the remainder of the division coming up, they were enabled to hold their position and soon
fortified it.

The Battle of Spotsylvania Courthouse, May 8th to 21st, 1864. The distance between the lines at this salient was less than two hundred yards. The desperate fighting of General Emory Upton's brigade caused it to be called the "Bloody Angle."

About 4 o'clock in the afternoon the assault was ordered. Warren's and Wright's Corps, with Mott's division of Hancock's corps to move simultaneously. The movement was prompt, and in a few minutes the fiercest of struggles began. The battlefield was so densely covered with forest little could be seen by any one person as to the progress made. Meade and I occupied the best position we could get, in rear of Warren.

The enemy was twice repulsed with heavy loss, though he had an entire corps against two brigades. Barlow took up his bridges in the presence of this force.

Desperate hand-to-hand fighting at the "Bloody Angle," the result of Hancock's division's surprise attack and capture of the salient.

Accordingly in the afternoon Hancock was ordered to move his command by the rear of Warren and Wright, under cover of night, to Wright's left, and there form it for an assault at 4 o'clock the next morning.

The ground, over which Hancock had to pass to reach the enemy, was ascending and heavily wooded to within two or three hundred yards of the enemy's intrenchments. In front of Birney there was also a marsh to cross. But notwithstanding all these difficulties, the troops pushed on in quick time without firing a gun, and when within four or five hundred yards of the enemy's line, broke out in loud cheers and, with a rush went up to and over the breastworks. Barlow and Birney entered almost simultaneously. Here a desperate hand-to-hand conflict took place. The men of the two sides were too close together to fire, but used their guns as clubs. The hand conflict was soon over. The victory was important, and one that Lee could not afford to leave us in full possession of.

General Grant reconnoitering the Confederate position at Spot-sylvania. From a sketch by Charles Reed, artist and soldier with Bigelow's 9th Massachusetts Battery, who saw Grant at the time.

Lee made the most strenuous efforts to regain the position he had lost. Five times during the day Lee assaulted furiously, but without dislodging our troops from their new position. His losses must have been fearful. It was three o'clock next morning before the firing ceased.

We were now to operate in a country different from any we had before seen in Virginia. The roads were wide and good, and the country well cultivated. No men were seen except those bearing arms, even the black men having been sent away. The country was new to us, and we had neither guides nor maps to tell us where the roads were or where they led to.

Crossing at Jericho Ford, on the North Anna River, used by the corps of Warren and Wright, May 24th to 26th, 1864.

Lee now had his entire army south of the North Anna. Our line covered his front, with the six miles separating the two wings guarded by but a single division. Lee had been reinforced, and was being reinforced, largely.

It was a delicate move to get the right wing of the Army of the Potomac from its position south of the North Anna in the presence of the enemy. On the 29th of May a reconnaissance was made in force to find Lee's position.

General Grant and "Cincinnati" in camp in Virginia. The photograph is a composite, Grant on horseback being mounted over the background picture.

Right: artillery battery resting in camp

Brigadier General Alfred Torbert and Staff.
General Torbert, the nattily dressed officer in the center of the
group wearing the white gauntlets, commanded a brigade under
General Philip Sheridan. Below: Brigadier General Wesley Mer-
ritt and Staff. General Merritt is seated second from the right. He
was one of the youngest cavalry generals in the Army.

General Grant and his cavalry commanders.

Major General Philip H. Sheridan,
Cavalry Commander, Army of the Potomac

Brigadier General Alfred Torbert

Brigadier General Wesley Merritt

Lieutenant General Ulysses S. Grant, Commander
in Chief of the Armies of the United States

Confederate prisoners captured at Spotsylvania, May 8–21, 1864

The night of May 30th, Lee's position was substantially from Atlee's Station, on the Virginia Central Railroad, south and east to the vicinity of Cold Harbor. The left of Warren's corps was on the Shady Grove Road, extending to the Mechanicsville Road, about three miles south of the Totopotomoy.

On the 30th Hancock moved to the Totopotomoy, where he found the enemy strongly fortified. There was some skirmishing along the center, and in the evening Early attacked Warren with some vigor, driving him back at first, and threatening to turn our left flank. While this was going on, Warren got his men up, repulsed Early, and drove him more than a mile.

Battle of Cold Harbor, Virginia, June 1st, 1864.

On the 31st of May, Sheridan advanced to near Old Cold Harbor. He found it intrenched and occupied by cavalry and infantry. A hard fight ensued but the place was carried. The enemy well knew the importance of Cold Harbor to us, and seemed determined that we should not hold it. Night came on before the enemy was ready for an assault.

An open plain intervened between the contending forces at this point, which was exposed both to a direct and a cross fire. This assault cost us heavily and probably without benefit to compensate; but the enemy was not cheered by the occurrence sufficiently to induce him to take the offensive.

Fighting was substantially over by half past seven in the morning.

During the night the enemy quitted our right front, abandoning some of their wounded, and without burying their dead. But there were many dead and wounded men between the lines of the contending forces, which were now close together, who could not be cared for without cessation of hostilities.

Forty-eight hours after it commenced parties were got out to collect the men left upon the field. In the meantime all but two of the wounded had died. I have always regretted that the last assault at Cold Harbor was ever made.

A dead Confederate soldier

Above: Grant and his favorite mount, "Cincinnati."
Right: Grant in front of his tent at Cold Harbor.

General Grant and Staff at City Point, Headquarters of the Army of the Potomac, July, 1864.

Seated, third from left, General John A. Rawlins, Chief of Staff. Grant sits next to the tree. To the right and left of the tent pole, General Asa Parker, Grant's full blooded Indian secretary, and General John Gross Barnard, Chief Engineer of the Army of the Potomac. Lieutenant Frederick Dent Grant, Grant's eldest son, stands directly behind General Parker.

Dahlgren gun mounted on siege carriage, James River, 1864.

CHAPTER XII

Petersburg: Bloody Stalemate

Lee's position was now so near Richmond, and the intervening swamps of the Chickahominy so great an obstacle to the movement of troops in the face of an enemy, that I determined to make my next left flank move carry the Army of the Potomac south of the James River. Preparations for this were promptly commenced. The move was a hazardous one to make. The Chickahominy River, with its marshy and heavily timbered approaches, had to be crossed, and all the bridges over it east of Lee were destroyed.

Lee, if he did not choose to follow me, might, with his shorter distance to travel and his bridges over the Chickahominy and the James, move rapidly on Butler and crush him before the army with me could come to his relief. But the move had to be made, and I relied upon Lee's not seeing my danger as I saw it.

[227]

Above: The swamps of the Chickahominy
Opposite: Ruins of Richmond railroad bridge

Richmond, Virginia, capital of the Confederacy in 1864.

Supplies were growing scarce in Richmond. The sources from which to draw them were in our hands. People from outside began to pour into Richmond to help eat up the little on hand. Consternation reigned there.

Besides we had armies on both sides of the James River and not far from the Confederate Capital. I knew that its safety would be a matter of the first consideration with the so-called Confederate Government, if it was not with the military commanders. But I took all the precaution I knew of to guard against all dangers.

Landing supplies for Grant's army on the James River, 1864

U.S. Navy double-ender gunboat in the James River guarding the landings below.

The advance of the Army of the Potomac reached the James River on the 14th of June, 1864. Preparations were at once commenced for laying the pontoon bridges and crossing the river. I had previously ordered General Butler to have two vessels loaded with stone and carried up the river to a point above that occupied by our gunboats, where the channel was narrow, and sunk there so as to obstruct the passage and prevent Confederate gunboats from coming down the river.

Up to this time Beauregard, who commanded south of Richmond, had received no reinforcements, except Hoke's division from Drury's Bluff, which had arrived on the morning of the 16th, though he had urged the authorities very strongly to send them, believing, as he did, that Petersburg would be a valuable prize which we might seek.

Battle of Petersburg, Virginia.
Attack on Beauregard's position, June 17, 1864.

During the 17th the fighting was very severe and the losses heavy. At night our troops occupied about the same position they had occupied in the morning, except that they held the redan which had been captured by Potter during the day.

During the night, Beauregard fell back to the line which had been already selected, and commenced fortifying it. On the 18th our troops advanced to the line which he had abandoned and found that the Confederate loss had been very severe, many of the enemy's dead still remaining in the ditches.

The Army of the Potomac was given the investment of Petersburg, while the Army of the James held Bermuda Hundred and all the ground we possessed north of the James River.

City Point on the James River. Main supply base and headquarters of General Grant.

General Grant's headquarters shack at City Point. Mathew Brady, the war photographer, in top hat and cane, stands behind General Rawlins, Grant's Chief of Staff. Grant is seated on Rawlins' left. Lieutenant Frederick Dent Grant, the General's eldest son, is seated second from right.

*The Civil War's "ultimate weapon,"
the giant Knox mortar "Dictator,"
and the "Petersburg Express,"
on Grant's City Point Railroad.*

*Officer's Quarters in the lines
before Petersburg. For nearly five
months, officers and men alike
lived in these bomb shelters.*

Mess cooks, City Point, Virginia

General Grant, Mrs. Grant and their youngest son, Jesse, at City Point. Both of General Grant's sons were no strangers to army life and war.

Below: cumbersome equipment of the army photographer. The wagon, with water buckets slung under the axle; tents for sleeping quarters; the all-important camera and chemicals, and darkroom tent in background. The officer leaning against the tree is believed to be Captain A. J. Russel, of the Signal Corps.

Above: A redan in the lines before Petersburg, June 1864. Mathew Brady, the war photographer, can be seen standing near the revetments, wearing a straw hat, his hand on his hip. Below: General Grant and Staff before Petersburg. His Chief of Staff, General John A. Rawlins, is seated farthest left. Lieutenant Frederick Dent Grant, the General's eldest son, is seated behind his father, wearing light trousers.

Above: Living the life of moles in underground bombproof shelters in the lines before Petersburg. Right: Battery of thirty-pounder Parrotts in a salient in the lines before Petersburg, July, 1864.

The 9th Corps, Burnside's, was placed on the right of Petersburg; the 5th, Warren's, next; the 2nd, Birney's, next; then the 6th, Wright's, broken off to the left and south. Thus began the siege of Petersburg.

After these events comparative quiet reigned about Petersburg until late in July. The time, however, was spent in strengthening the intrenchments and making our position generally more secure against a sudden attack.

[235]

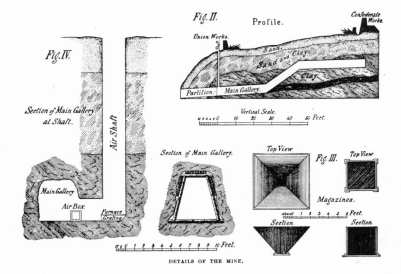

Fig. II. Profile. Confederate Works.

Fig. IV.

Section of Main Gallery at Shaft.

Air Shaft.

Main Gallery.

Air Box. Furnace Grating.

Section of Main Gallery.

Top View. Fig. III. Top View.

Magazines.

Section. Section.

DETAILS OF THE MINE.

Diagram of the mine under the Confederate works in side view. Below, left: Gallery of the mine. Below, right: Entrance to the mine gallery.

Outline of Crater.
S. 8° E.
Course of Confederate Works.
Magazines.
Magazines.
Outline of Crater.

On the 25th of June, General Burnside had commenced running a mine from about the center of his front under the Confederate works confronting him. He was induced to do this by Colonel Pleasants, of the Pennsylvania Volunteers, whose regiment was mostly composed of miners. Burnside had submitted this scheme to Meade and myself, and we both approved of it as a means of keeping the men occupied.

The position of the two lines at that point were only about a hundred yards apart with a comparatively deep ravine intervening. The mine was ordered to be charged, and the morning of the 30th of July was the time fixed for its explosion.

The gallery to the mine was over five hundred feet long from where it entered the ground to the point where it was under the enemy's works, and with a cross gallery of something over eighty feet running under their lines.

Explosion of the mine under the Confederate trenches. Below: Battle in The Crater, between the men of Ledlie's Division and Wright's Brigade of Mahone's Division.

There was some delay about the explosion of the mine so that it did not go off until about five o'clock in the morning. When it did explode it was very successful, making a crater twenty feet deep and something like a hundred feet in length.

Ledlie's division marched into the crater immediately on the explosion, but most of the men stopped there in the absence of anyone to give directions; their commander having found some safe retreat to get into before they started.

The effort was a stupendous failure. It cost us about four thousand men, mostly captured; all due to the incompetency of the division commander who was sent to lead the assault.

[237]

General Grant at headquarters, City
Point. Left to right: Brigadier General
John A. Rawlins, Grant, and Colonel
Theodore Bowers.

Alexander H. Stevens, Vice President
of the Confederacy, 1864.

Sheridan met Early at the crossing of the Opequon Creek, and won a most decisive victory, one which electrified the country. Early had invited this attack himself by his bad generalship, and made the victory easy.

On the last of January, 1865, the peace commissioners from the so-called Confederate States presented themselves on our lines around Petersburg, and were immediately conducted to my headquarters at City Point. They proved to be Alexander H. Stevens, Vice President of the Confederacy; Judge Campbell, Assistant Secretary of War; and R. M. T. Hunter, formerly United States Senator, and then a member of the Confederate Senate.

President Lincoln and his son, Tad, visit General Grant at City Point, 1864. Winslow Homer, artist for Harper's Weekly, *made this sketch. Above; left: Senator R. M. T. Hunter, of the Confederate States. Below, left: General Lew Wallace*

I at once communicated by telegraph with Washington and informed the Secretary of War and the President of the arrival of these commissioners and that their object was to negotiate terms of peace.

About the 2nd of February I received a dispatch from Washington, directing me to send the commissioners to Hampton Roads to meet the President and a member of the Cabinet.

It was not a great while after they met that the President visited me at City Point. He spoke of having met the commissioners, and said that he had told them that there would be no use in entering into any negotiations unless they would recognize, first: that the Union as a whole must be forever preserved, and second: that slavery must be abolished.

Union battery near the Dunn House in the lines before Petersburg, 1864. The civilian standing on the fuse boxes is Mathew Brady (center), the war photographer.

One of the most anxious periods of my experience during the rebellion was the last few weeks before Petersburg. I was afraid every morning that I would awake from my sleep to hear that Lee had gone, and that nothing was left but a picket line.

I had, as early as the 1st of March, given instructions around Petersburg to keep a sharp lookout to see that such a movement should not escape their notice, and to be ready to strike at once if it was undertaken.

Finally, on the 29th of March, I moved out with all the army available after leaving sufficient force to hold the line about Petersburg. The next day, March 30th, we had made sufficient progress to the southwest to warrant me in starting Sheridan with his cavalry over by Dinwiddie with instructions to then come up by the road leading northwest to Five Forks, thus menacing the right of Lee's line.

Inviting a shot in the Confederate lines, Petersburg, 1864.

It is now known that early in the month of March, Mr. Davis and General Lee had a consultation about the situation of affairs in and about Richmond and Petersburg, and they both agreed that these places were no longer tenable for them, and that they must get away as soon as possible.

During the night of April 2nd, our line was intrenched from the river above to the river below. I ordered a bombardment to be commenced the next morning at 5 A.M. to be followed by an assault at 6 o'clock, but the enemy evacuated Petersburg early in the morning.

As expected, Lee's troops had moved during the night before, and our army in moving upon Amelia Court House soon encountered them.

The armies finally met at Sailor's Creek, where a heavy engagement took place, in which infantry, artillery and cavalry were all brought into action. The enemy's loss was very heavy. Lee's army was rapidly crumbling.

Prisoners from the front, Petersburg, 1864. The young officer receiving the prisoners is Brigadier General Francis C. Barlow.

Sheridan sent Custer with his division to move south of Appomattox Station, which is about five miles southwest of the courthouse, to get west of Lee's trains and destroy the roads to the rear. So far, only our cavalry and the advance of Lee's army were engaged.

Soon Lee's men were brought from the rear, no doubt expecting they had nothing to meet but our cavalry. But our infantry pushed forward so rapidly that by the time the enemy got up they found the Army of the James confronting them. A sharp engagement ensued, but Lee quickly set up a white flag.

When the white flag was put out by Lee, I was moving towards Appomattox Court House, and consequently could not be communicated with immediately, and be informed of what Lee had done.

*The McLean House, Appomattox Courthouse, Virginia, April 9th,
1865, scene of Lee's surrender of the Army of Northern Virginia.*

I found him at the house of a Mr. McLean, at Appomattox Court
House, with Colonel Marshall, one of his staff officers, awaiting my
arrival. General Lee was dressed in full uniform which was entirely
new, and was wearing a sword of considerable value, very likely
the sword which had been presented by the State of Virginia.

In my rough travelling suit, the uniform of a private with the
straps of a lieutenant general, I must have contrasted very strangely
with a man so handsomely dressed, six feet high and of faultless
form. We soon fell into conversation about old army times. Our
conversation was so pleasant I almost forgot the object of our meeting. This continued for some time when General Lee again inter-
rupted the course of the conversation by suggesting that the terms
I proposed to give his army ought to be written out. General Lee,
after all was completed, remarked that his army was in a very bad
condition for want of food, and that they were without forage.

Lee surrenders the Army of Northern Virginia, April 9, 1865, 4:30 p.m. Lee, resplendent in a new uniform, writes at a small table. Grant and his officers watch quietly. General Sheridan stands against the wall on the right. Colonel Marshall, Lee's aide, stands in front of the fireplace.

Lee and I then separated as cordially as we had met, he returning to his own lines, and all went into bivouac for the night at Appomattox. Soon after Lee's departure I telegraphed to Washington as follows:

HEADQUARTERS, APPOMATTOX COURTHOUSE, VA.
April 9th, 1865, 4:30 P.M.

HON. E. M. STANTON, SECRETARY OF WAR
WASHINGTON.

General Lee surrendered the Army of Northern Virginia this afternoon on terms proposed by myself. The accompanying additional correspondence will show the conditions fully.

U. S. GRANT,

LIEUT. GENERAL.

Appomattox Courthouse, Virginia, at the time of Lee's surrender,
April 9th, 1865

The trench complex of
Petersburg. The soldiers have
gone. The fields are silent,
except for the sounds of
birds. The war is over.

Richmond, the Confederacy's citadel in ruins, 1865.

End of a lost cause

Acknowledgments

GRATEFUL acknowledgment is made to the following professional people for their kind assistance in the preparation of this book:

To my friend and colleague William Kaland, of the Westinghouse Broadcasting Company, a Civil War enthusiast and collector, I extend my thanks for his contribution of the preface.

To Mrs. Francis Stager for the final typing of the edited manuscript; and to my son, Arthur, for his design of the jacket and the performing of necessary errands and research of the hard-to-find pictures.

I am also indebted to my friend Professor Robert M. Langdon, of the United States Naval Academy at Annapolis, for his valuable assistance in searching for the important pictures of the naval actions of the Mexican War belonging to the Admiral Walke collection of the Academy library.

I am also greatly indebted to Colonel Frederick Porter Todd, Director of the West Point Museum, for his assistance in locating several rare pictures of the Academy in Grant's time; and to Mr. Emil Weiss, Assistant Librarian, for his kind assistance in searching for rare prints and photographs for the West Point sequence.

I also extend my grateful appreciation to Mr. Richard Hagen, of the State of Illinois Department of Monuments and Memorials, for his efforts in locating rare photographs of Grant's home town of Galena.

Finally, to Anne Whitman Meredith I extend my grateful appreciation for assistance in preparing the illustrations for publication.

ROY MEREDITH

New York, May, 1959

Contributing Institutions and Historical Societies

THE author wishes to acknowledge the generous help and cooperation afforded him by the following institutions and historical societies in the preparation of the book:

United States Military Academy, West Point, New York.

United States Naval Academy, Annapolis, Maryland.

Department of the Army, Office of the Chief of Military History, Washington, D.C.

Department of Monuments and Memorials, State Capitol, Springfield, Illinois.

The Metropolitan Museum of Art, New York City.

The Detroit Museum of Art, Detroit, Michigan.

The New York Public Library, Stokes Collection.

Victor D. Spark Galleries, New York.

M. Knoedler & Company Galleries, New York.

Culver Service, New York.

The New York Historical Society, New York.

Robert Vose Galleries, Boston, Massachusetts.

The Pennsylvania Railroad.

Note: The Civil War photographs are from the David B. Woodbury collection, made in Virginia during Grant's campaign by Woodbury in 1864–1865, and are the property of the editor.

Index

OVERLEAF: *Battery "D", 5th United States Artillery*

DATE DUE

JAN 11			
1/28			
11-1-04			